i Can Speak

3 Red

An integrated course for communicative success

Pagoda Language Education Center

PAGODA Books

Copyright © 2011 by **PAGODA Books**

All rights reserved. No part of this publication may be reproduced, stored in a retrieval system, or transmitted, in any form, or by any means, electronic, mechanical, photocopying, recording or otherwise, without the prior written permission of the copyright holder and the publisher.

Published by PAGODA Books

PAGODA Books is the professional language publishing company of the
PAGODA Education Group.
19F, PAGODA Tower, 419, Gangnam-daero,
Seocho-gu, Seoul, 06614, Rep. of KOREA
www.pagodabook.com

First published 2011
Sixteenth impression 2023
Printed in the Republic of Korea

ISBN 978-89-6281-247-3 (14740)

Publisher | Kyung-Sil Park
Writer | PAGODA Language Education Center

Acknowledgements

Thanks to the following for their contributions in providing us feedback:
Sue Ahn, Ahmi Cha, Jessica Han, Cindy Jung, Amber Kang, Ella Kim, Grace Kim, Christina Lee, Joanne Lee, Kacey Lee, Kay Lim, Mia Lim, Sooji Park, Rachel Shin, Rose Shin

A defective book may be exchanged at the store where you purchased it.

Introduction

What is *i* Can Speak?

i Can Speak is a three-level, six-book series designed to develop English speaking skills. Levels 1 through 3 cover the elementary, pre-intermediate, and intermediate levels, respectively. The books focus on real-life communication, presenting learners with realistic scenarios and engaging, relevant activities. Aside from developing speaking skills, *i* Can Speak 3 Red also includes reading, writing, and listening activities to help intermediate students become all-round communicators.

How is the book organized?

Each lesson includes:

- A **Warm-Up** activity, which activates learners' knowledge of the lesson's theme and gets the class talking straight away
- Two **dialogues**, which present the lesson's theme and language points within real-life contexts
- **Language Focus** boxes, which highlight key language from dialogues for learners to use in the following speaking activities
- Three graded **Talk** speaking activities, which allow learners to practice and personalize the lesson's language focus. Some **Talk** activities also include listening practice.
- *i* **Read** – an opportunity for learners to react to written stimulus based on the lesson's theme
- *i* **Write** – an activity that gives learners the chance to express themselves in writing, using the lesson's theme and language focus

What is included with the book?

The book is accompanied by:

- An **audio CD** containing all the listening material from the book
- A **Mini Book**, which includes the dialogues and pronunciation material from each lesson, as well as a Wordlist for every lesson
- **MP3 files** downloadable from www.pagodabook.com

Scope and Sequence

Introduction ---------------------------- 3
Key to Phonetic Symbols ---------------- 6
Table of Irregular Verbs ---------------- 7
Classroom Language ---------------------- 8

	Theme	Language Focus	Page
Lesson 1 Let me introduce you to my classmate, Cindy.	Getting to Know People	• Greetings and Responses	10
Lesson 2 Thanksgiving is next week!	Holidays and Traditions	• Talking About Holiday Foods • Expressing Interest • Making Comparisons	18
Lesson 3 I'm extremely romantic.	Personality	• Opposite Adjectives • Opposite Adjectives With Prefixes (*im-*, *un-*, *dis-*, *in-*) • Questions About Personality • Discussing Ideal Personalities • More Adjectives	26
Lesson 4 Are you feeling OK?	Feelings and Emotions	• Talking About Feelings • Fixed Expressions for Feelings • Making Suggestions • Cheering People Up	34
Lesson 5 Why don't you go see a doctor?	Illness	• Giving Advice 1 • Giving Advice 2	42
Lesson 6 People say it's the best in the world.	Choosing the Best	• Comparing Things • Asking for and Giving Opinions	50
Lesson 7 You look gorgeous in those skinny jeans.	Healthy Living	• Staying in Shape • Losing Weight	58
Lesson 8 Do you do a lot of exercise?	Exercise and Healthy Eating	• Talking About Frequency	66

	Theme	Language Focus	Page
Lesson 9 Have you ever tried Mexican food?	In the Past	• Life Experiences • Effects of Past Actions • Things That Began in the Past and Continue Until Now	74
Lesson 10 Where shall we go on vacation this year?	Travel	• Reserving a Flight • Making Suggestions / Planning • Agreeing • Disagreeing	82
Lesson 11 What did it taste like?	Food and Eating Customs Around the World	• Asking for Information and Making Comparisons • Likes and Dislikes • Talking About What You Have Learned	90
Lesson 12 Hello. Is Tim there?	Using the Telephone	• Formal Telephone Language • Informal Telephone Language	98
Lesson 13 I'd like to make an appointment for a haircut.	Appointments	• Making Appointments 1 • Making Appointments 2	106
Lesson 14 I think we have some problems.	Problems	• Requests and Replies • Complaining and Responding to Complaints	114
Lesson 15 How old were you?	Memories and Past Events	• Life History 1 • Life History 2	122
Lesson 16 Are you going to change your career?	Into the Future	• Future Plans	130
Listening Scripts			138

Key to Phonetic Symbols

Consonants

/p/	park	/ŋ/	sing	/z/	rise
/t/	time	/f/	laugh	/ʒ/	vision
/k/	cat	/θ/	thing	/dʒ/	page
/b/	rob	/s/	rice	/w/	want
/d/	road	/ʃ/	action	/r/	ride
/g/	go	/tʃ/	church	/l/	live
/m/	make	/v/	very	/j/	use
/n/	rain	/ð/	those	/h/	here

Vowels

/ɪ/	sit	/e/	any	/ɑ/	on	/ɔɪ/	boy
/iː/	seat	/ɜː/	early	/ɑː/	arm	/eə/	area
/uː/	you	/ɔː/	sport	/ɪə/	near	/əʊ/	over
/ə/	arrive	/æ/	apple	/ʊə/	tour	/aɪ/	eye
/ʊ/	good	/ʌ/	umbrella	/eɪ/	face	/aʊ/	cow

Table of Irregular Verbs

Base Form	Simple Past	Past Participle	Base Form	Simple Past	Past Participle
be	was/were	been	let	let	let
beat	beat	beaten	lie	lay	lain
become	became	become	light	lit	lit
begin	began	begun	lose	lost	lost
bite	bit	bitten	make	made	made
blow	blew	blown	mean	meant	meant
break	broke	broken	meet	met	met
bring	brought	brought	pay	paid	paid
build	built	built	put	put	put
buy	bought	bought	read	read	read
catch	caught	caught	ride	rode	ridden
choose	chose	chosen	ring	rang	rung
come	came	come	rise	rose	risen
cost	cost	cost	run	ran	run
cut	cut	cut	say	said	said
do	did	done	see	saw	seen
draw	drew	drawn	sell	sold	sold
drink	drank	drunk	send	sent	sent
drive	drove	driven	shine	shone	shone
eat	ate	eaten	shoot	shot	shot
fall	fell	fallen	show	showed	shown/showed
feel	felt	felt	shut	shut	shut
fight	fought	fought	sing	sang	sung
find	found	found	sit	sat	sat
fly	flew	flown	sleep	slept	slept
forget	forgot	forgotten	speak	spoke	spoken
get	got	gotten	spend	spent	spent
give	gave	given	stand	stood	stood
go	went	gone	steal	stole	stolen
grow	grew	grown	swim	swam	swum
hang	hung	hung	take	took	taken
have	had	had	teach	taught	taught
hear	heard	heard	tear	tore	torn
hide	hid	hidden	tell	told	told
hit	hit	hit	think	thought	thought
hold	held	held	throw	threw	thrown
hurt	hurt	hurt	understand	understood	understood
keep	kept	kept	wake	woke	woken
know	knew	known	wear	wore	worn
leave	left	left	win	won	won
lend	lent	lent	write	wrote	written

Classroom Language

Teacher Talk

Student Talk

Lesson 1

Let me introduce you to my classmate, Cindy.

Warm-Up

A Read the information about greetings in different countries around the world. Match the countries with the greetings.

Greetings Around the World

① To say 'hello' and 'goodbye' here, people kiss.

② Men often hug each other. Or, they shake hands.

③ People shake hands firmly and make direct eye contact.

④ Some people greet each other by rubbing noses.

⑤ People place their hands in a praying position and bow slightly.

⑥ Here people shake hands firmly, hug, and then kiss two or three times.

⑦ Here you should bow your head to greet people.

Brazil   India   Japan   Italy
Russia   New Zealand   USA

B Do you know of any other greetings in other countries? Tell the class about them.

Dialogue 1 — Listen to the dialogue and practice.

Brian: Hi, Ellen! How's it going?
Ellen: Pretty good, and you?
Brian: Not bad. Actually, I'm very busy with an essay.
Ellen: Oh, I see. Let me introduce you to my classmate, Cindy. She's from Canada. Cindy, this is my friend, Brian. He's from England.
Brian: Nice to meet you, Cindy.
Cindy: Nice to meet you, too, Brian.
Brian: Where in Canada do you live?
Cindy: I live in Vancouver. I was born there.
Brian: I've been to Vancouver. My cousin lives in North Vancouver. It's a beautiful place.
Cindy: It sure is. I love my hometown.
Brian: Well, let's get together for lunch sometime, OK?
Ellen: Sure, Brian. Take care. Bye!

Comprehension Check!

1. Who does Brian already know?
2. Who does Brian meet for the first time?
3. Where is Cindy from?

Language Focus

Greetings and Responses

Glad to meet you.	Nice to meet you, too. / Glad to meet you, too.
Brian, **I'd like you to meet my friend,** Cindy.	Nice to meet you, Cindy.
Cindy, **let me introduce you to my friend,** Brian.	Glad to meet you, Brian.
How are you? / How are you doing?	Great. / Pretty good. / Fine, thanks. / OK. / Not bad.
How's it going? / How are things going?	So-so. / Terrible.
What's up?	Not much. / Nothing much.
What's new?	**I'm busy with** a presentation.
What do you do?	**I'm an** accountant.
Where are you from?	**I'm from** England.
Where do you come from?	**I come from** England.
When were you born?	**I was born on** October 2, 1978.
What do you like to do in your free time?	I like to go for walks.

Talk 1

 Ask three classmates questions to complete the table.

Example
A: Hi, what's your name?
B: My name's Carrie Kim.
A: Nice to meet you, Carrie. My name's Robert.
B: Glad to meet you, too, Robert. What's your surname?
⋮

	Classmate 1	Classmate 2	Classmate 3
Surname			
First Name			
Occupation			
Address			
Date of Birth			
Marital Status			
Nationality			

B Introduce the three classmates to other classmates.

Example: Ben, I'd like you to meet Carrie Kim. Carrie's an assistant manager in a cargo company.

continue

Pronunciation

Syllables

Discover Pronunciation!
English words are made of smaller sounds called syllables.
Hi (= 1 syllable)
Busy (= 2 syllables)
Canada (= 3 syllables)

Practice Pronunciation!
Listen to the words from Dialogue 1. Write the number of syllables in each word. Then practice saying the words with your partner.

1. good
2. essay
3. introduce
4. classmate
5. friend
6. meet
7. England
8. Vancouver
9. sure
10. hometown

Dialogue 2
Listen to the dialogue and practice.

Simon: Hello, I'm Simon. Glad to meet you.
Jenny: Hi, I'm Jenny. Glad to meet you, too.
Simon: Which department do you work in?
Jenny: I work in the Accounting Department. What about you?
Simon: I work in the Human Resources Department. What exactly do you do there?
Jenny: I'm a bookkeeper. What kind of work do you do in your department?
Simon: I hire people, organize interviews, that kind of thing. So, what do you like to do after work?
Jenny: I usually go home, make dinner, and go out for a walk. How about you?
Simon: I always go to the gym and work out. Sometimes I go jogging in the park, too.
Jenny: Well, it was nice talking to you. Keep up the good work!
Simon: Same to you, Jenny! Take care!

Comprehension Check!
1. What do Simon and Jenny do?
2. What do they like to do in their free time?

Talk 2

A Simon asks Jenny more questions. Complete the questions with your partner, using the appropriate words from the box.

| where | do you | how many | what kind of |

1. _____ _____ live? — I live near downtown.
2. _____ people do you live with? — I live with four people: my parents and my two sisters.
3. _____ have any pets? — Yes, I have a cat.
4. _____ like movies? — Yes, I love movies.
5. _____ movies do you like? — I like horror movies.
6. _____ go to school? — No, I work full time.
7. _____ food do you like? — I really like Italian food.

B Practice asking and answering the questions in **A** with your partner.

Example
A: Carrie, how many people do you live with?
B: I live with my parents. My sister got married and left home.

continue

Lesson 1 · 15

Talk 3

A Ask your classmates questions to complete the table. Whoever completes five sets of information first is the winner.

Example
A: Do you live alone?
B: Yes, I do.

A: Where do you live?
B: About 20 minutes from here.

FIND SOMEONE WHO ...

lives alone	likes romantic movies	speaks Japanese	works in an office
Name: Details:	Name: Details:	Name: Details:	Name: Details:
has a pet	**lives near a subway station**	**has visited another country**	**has a car**
Name: Details:	Name: Details:	Name: Details:	Name: Details:
has two brothers	**goes to a gym**	**lives with at least one grandparent**	**speaks a European language**
Name: Details:	Name: Details:	Name: Details:	Name: Details:
has a smartphone	**plays a musical instrument**	**plays sports**	**goes jogging regularly**
Name: Details:	Name: Details:	Name: Details:	Name: Details:

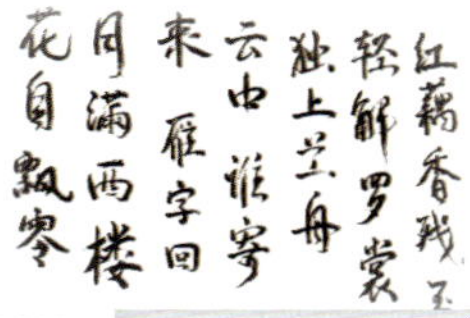

B Tell your partner what you found out about your other classmates.

Example
Jennifer plays a musical instrument. She plays the piano.

i Read

A Read the advertisements. Why did the people write the advertisements?

Looking for a Friend

I am a 24-year-old female. I am an exchange student from Europe. I have a few friends but would like to have some more. I love outdoor activities, shopping, cooking, and watching movies. If you would like to meet up, drop me a line at myfriend@coolmail.com.

Language Exchange

I'm a 27-year-old Mexican male, looking for language exchange. I can read and write in English, but I am not good at speaking. I really want to speak well! I speak Spanish, and French because my mom is French. If you are interested, please contact me at julio1@umail.com.

B Discuss the questions with your partner.

1. What does the writer of the first advertisement like doing?
2. How well does the writer of the second advertisement speak English?
3. Which advertisement would you choose to respond to? Why?

i Write

A Read the e-mail from Akiko to her e-pal. What does Akiko say about herself in the e-mail?

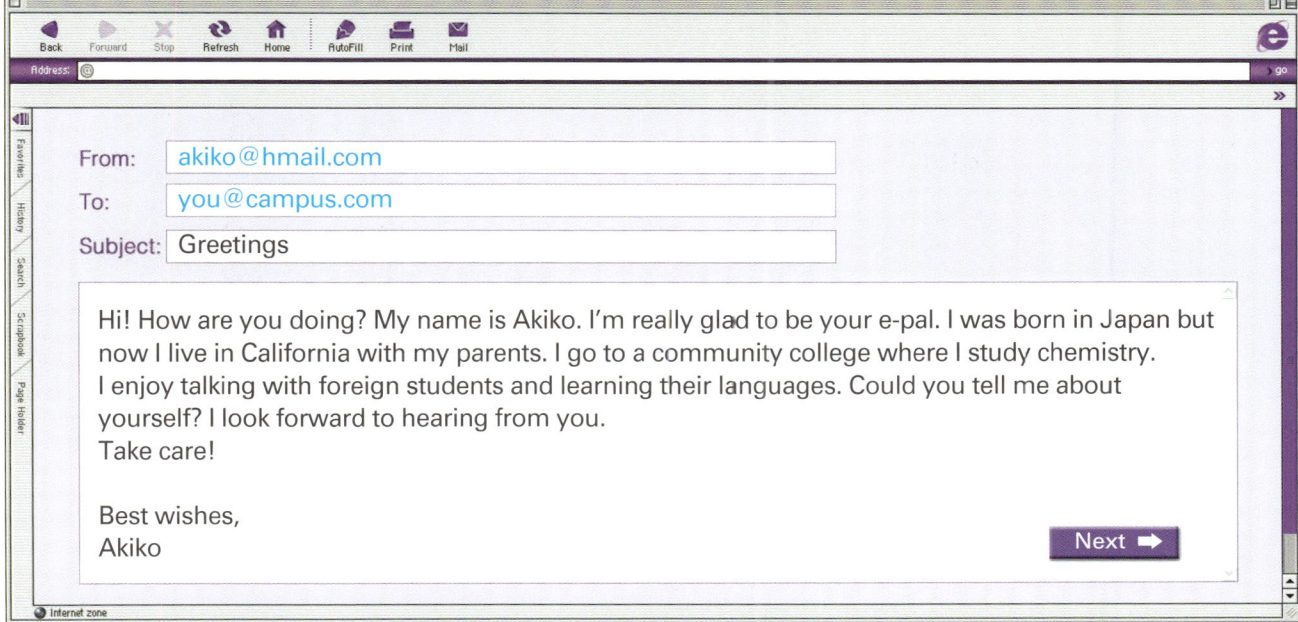

From: akiko@hmail.com
To: you@campus.com
Subject: Greetings

Hi! How are you doing? My name is Akiko. I'm really glad to be your e-pal. I was born in Japan but now I live in California with my parents. I go to a community college where I study chemistry. I enjoy talking with foreign students and learning their languages. Could you tell me about yourself? I look forward to hearing from you.
Take care!

Best wishes,
Akiko

B Write a reply to Akiko to introduce yourself to her.

Lesson 2: Thanksgiving is next week!

Warm-Up

A Match the holidays and traditions with the pictures.

Famous Holidays and Traditions

Fourth of July picnic	New Year's Eve	Valentine's Day
Halloween	Easter procession	Christmas

B What do you know about the holidays and traditions in **A**? Talk with your classmates.

Dialogue 1  *Listen to the dialogue and practice.*

James: Hi, Sarah! Thanksgiving is next week! I can hardly wait to visit my parents.
Sarah: Oh, yes. You're going to New York to see your family, aren't you? How exciting!
James: What about you? Are you visiting your family?
Sarah: Yes. My family lives close by, so I'm going to spend some time with them. I'm going to help my mom cook Thanksgiving dinner.
James: That sounds great. I love Thanksgiving dinner. Roast turkey, stuffing, mashed potatoes with gravy, cranberry sauce, casserole, yam …
Sarah: And for dessert? What's your favorite dessert?
James: My favorite dessert has got to be homemade pumpkin pie. My mom bakes it with fresh pumpkin. There's nothing like it!
Sarah: My mouth is watering! Well, it's time for class. I'll talk to you later.
James: All right. See you later!

Comprehension Check!
1. What are James and Sarah going to do at Thanksgiving?
2. What Thanksgiving traditions do they describe?

Language Focus 1

Talking About Holiday Foods

What's your favorite holiday food?	I like/love/adore eating pumpkin pie at Thanksgiving. My favorite has got to be picnic food on the Fourth of July.
What do you most like eating at Christmas?	I most like eating turkey at Christmas. It's got to be turkey.
What's your favorite dessert?	My favorite dessert is Christmas pudding.
What's pumpkin pie made of?	It's made of pumpkin, sugar, eggs, milk, ginger, and some spices.

Talk 1

Talk with your partner about your favorite holiday foods.

> **Example**
> A: What's your favorite holiday food?
> B: It's got to be apple pie.
> A: Oh, really? What's it made of?
> B: It's made of apples, flour, sugar, and spices.

Dialogue 2
Listen to the dialogue and practice.

Maria: Hi, Steve! What are you doing? What are all those books for?
Steve: Hello! I'm doing some research on world holidays for my anthropology class. It's so interesting.
Maria: Great. I'd like to know more about different customs around the world. Can you tell me about your research?
Steve: Sure. For example, Koreans celebrate New Year's Day twice. They have Western New Year's Day and Lunar New Year's Day.
Maria: Really? I didn't know that. Is there any difference between the two?
Steve: Yes. On January 1, people just take a day off and rest. Lunar New Year's Day, on the other hand, lasts for three days. Many people return to their hometowns to visit their families.
Maria: Wow, how interesting! Please tell me more about Lunar New Year's Day. Do Korean people do anything else during that holiday?
Steve: Yes. Many people wear traditional colorful dress. They bow to their parents and grandparents.

Comprehension Check!
1. What does Steve say about Lunar New Year's Day?
2. How is Lunar New Year's Day different from Western New Year's Day?

Language Focus 2

Expressing Interest

I'd like to know more about Christmas in Europe.
Please tell me more about Christmas traditions in your country.
I'm curious to know more about what people eat on that day.
I'm interested in different traditions around the world.
Wow, how interesting!
Really? I didn't know that.
That sounds interesting.

Talk 2

 Complete the table with information about four holidays in your country.

Holiday	Date	Traditions

B Imagine that your partner is a visitor to your country. Roleplay a conversation, using the information in **A**.

Example
- **A:** Do you have any questions about living in this country?
- **B:** Yes, I'd like to know more about traditions here. What's the next holiday?
- **A:** It's Thanksgiving.
- **B:** That sounds interesting. Could you tell me about it?
- **A:** Sure.

Language Focus 3

Making Comparisons

What's the difference between Christmas in western countries and in Asian countries**?**
Is there any difference between the two?
What makes them different?
What are the differences and similarities?
I think it's quite similar (to …).
It's totally different.
Yes, there are some big differences. For example, …
Christmas is **more important in** Europe **than in** Asian countries.
Lunar New Year is celebrated throughout Asia. In Europe, **on the other hand,** Lunar New Year is not a traditional celebration.

Talk 3

Talk with your partner about the similarities and differences between the holidays in your country and in other countries.

Valentine's Day is quite similar in my country to in other countries, but there are some differences. For example, men don't give gifts to women. Only women give gifts on Valentine's Day.

1. New Year's Eve
2. Valentine's Day
3. Halloween
4. Easter
5. Christmas
6. Thanksgiving

i Read

A Read the information about holidays around the world. What do you find most interesting about each holiday?

• Groundhog Day

Country	USA
Date	February 2
Significance	The groundhog awakens on February 2 and leaves its burrow. If it sees its shadow and goes back into its burrow, winter will last six more weeks. If the groundhog remains outside, spring begins.
Traditions	Groundhog Day is officially observed in Punxsutawney, Pennsylvania. People watch a groundhog leaving its burrow and see whether it sees its shadow. The people then announce the result.

• Thai Water Festival (*Songkran*)

Country	Thailand
Date	April 13 (duration 3–10 days)
Significance	*Songkran* marks the beginning of a new solar year. The festival started about 1,000 years ago to celebrate the farming season. Thai people believe that water washes away bad luck. Families gather and pour scented water onto the hands of their older relatives. They also give them gifts. In return, older relatives wish younger people good luck and prosperity.
Traditions	People use buckets, water guns, hoses, and even elephants to drench their family, friends, neighbors, and passers-by. There are also beauty pageants, traditional dances, and performances.

• Cinco de Mayo

Country	Mexico (Puebla), USA
Date	May 5
Significance	Cinco de Mayo celebrates the victory of 4,000 Mexican soldiers over 8,000 French fighters in the Battle of Puebla on May 5, 1862. It is a regional holiday in Mexico, and it is also celebrated in the USA and in other countries around the world where Mexicans live. It has become a celebration of Mexican heritage and pride.
Traditions	Many communities hold events that include Mexican singing, dancing, food with beer or tequila, parades, carnivals, street fairs, and festivals.

B Discuss the questions with your partner.
1. Which of the holidays in **A** do you find the most interesting? Why?
2. In your country, do you celebrate any similar holidays?

i Write

Write sentences to answer the questions.

1. What was your favorite holiday when you were young?
2. What holidays do you look forward to now? Why do you like them?
3. Describe one special food that you love to eat during a holiday.

Pronunciation

Identifying Word Stress

Discover Pronunciation!
Listen to the words from Dialogue 1 and Dialogue 2. Notice the way the speakers stress different syllables in the words. Practice saying the words, paying attention to the stressed syllables.

●	● ●	● ●	● ● ●	● ● ●
cook	pumpkin	July	procession	cranberry

When you learn a new word, it is useful to learn which syllable is stressed. This will help you pronounce the word correctly.

Practice Pronunciation!
Listen to some more words. Write the words in the correct columns. Then practice saying the words with your partner.

●	● ●	● ●	● ● ●	● ● ●

Lesson 3

I'm extremely romantic.

Warm-Up

A Match the descriptions with the adjectives.

What are you like?

1. I always tell the truth.
2. I usually feel happy.
3. I like meeting new people.
4. I give expensive gifts to my friends.
5. I'm good at making decisions.
6. I don't get angry when I have to wait for something.
7. The way I talk never upsets people.
8. I always do well in exams.
9. If I tell someone I'm going to do something, I do it.
10. I listen to other people's ideas and views.

a. patient
b. honest
c. reliable
d. outgoing
e. open-minded
f. generous
g. smart
h. polite
i. positive
j. decisive

generous  | outgoing  | smart

B Discuss the questions with your partner.
1. What kind of people do you like? Why?
2. Do you think personality is important? Why / Why not?
3. Are you happy with your personality? Why / Why not?

Dialogue 1 Listen to the dialogue and practice.

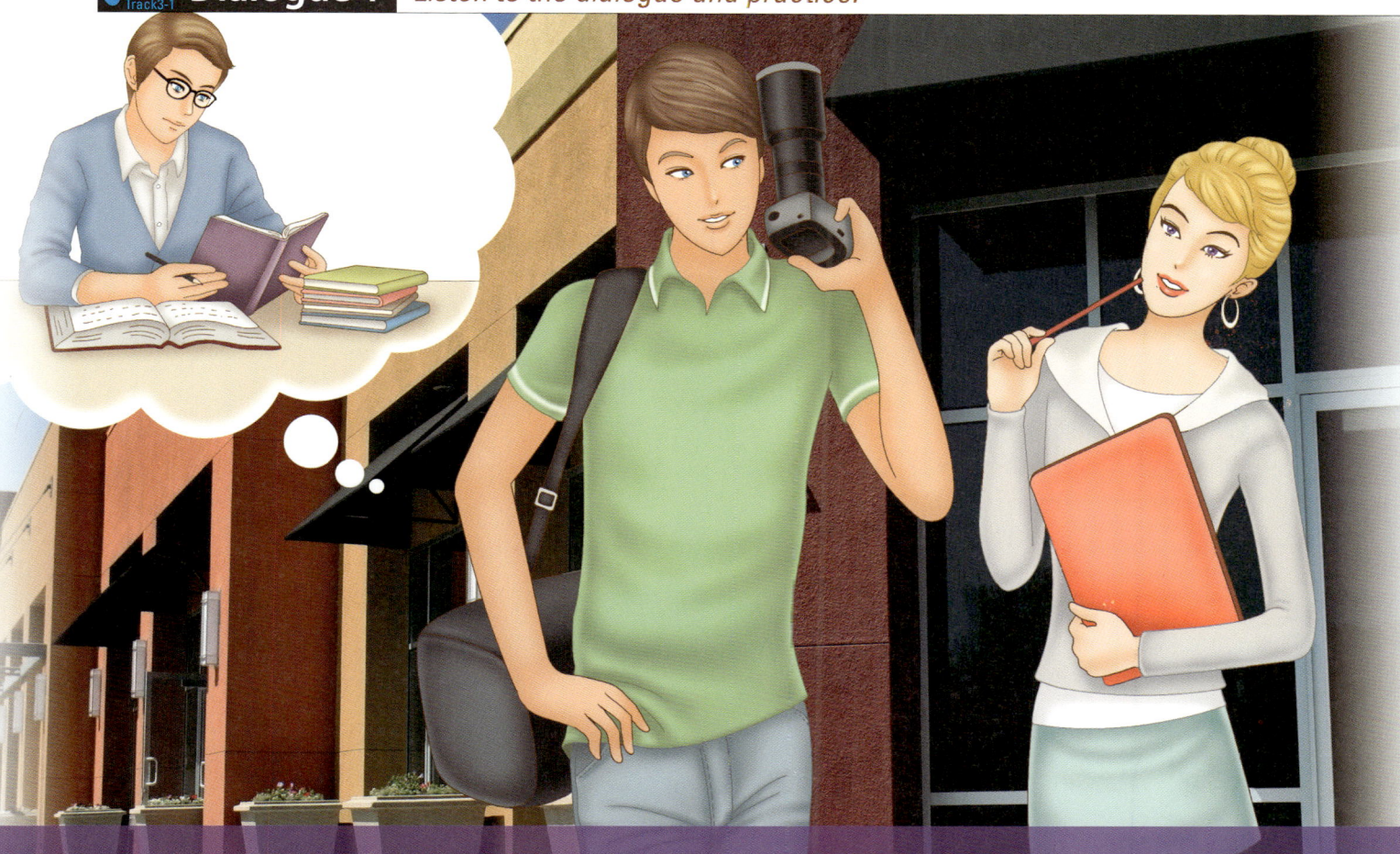

Tim: Hi, Sue. One of my friends at college, Mark, is looking for a new girlfriend. Are you interested in meeting him?
Sue: Um, I'm not sure. You know I don't like meeting new people. What's he like?
Tim: Well, I think he's honest and reliable. He always keeps my secrets! Also, he's generous. He gave me a fantastic MP3 player for my birthday last week. He is a little impatient though. If you're late, he won't wait!
Sue: Hmm … but is he very outgoing? My last boyfriend wanted to party all the time, and I didn't like it. He was also dishonest. I couldn't trust him. And he was unreliable. He often cancelled our dates at the last minute. Also, he never gave me any gifts. He was so mean! The worst thing of all though was that he was so impolite. He never said thank you!
Tim: Well, Mark isn't like that. He's quite shy. The only bad thing about him is that he's really indecisive!
Sue: Well, I'm good at making decisions. OK, I'll meet him.
Tim: Great!

Comprehension Check!

1. What are Sue and Mark like?
2. Do you think Sue and Mark will get along?
3. What was Sue's ex-boyfriend like?

Language Focus 1

Opposite Adjectives

smart	→	stupid
positive	→	negative
outgoing	→	shy
generous	→	mean

Opposite Adjectives With Prefixes
(*im-, un-, dis-, in-*)

honest	→	dishonest
patient	→	impatient
reliable	→	unreliable
polite	→	impolite
decisive	→	indecisive

Questions About Personality

What are you like? What's your personality like? What kind of person are you?	**I'm** outgoing.
What's he/she like?	**He's/She's** generous.
What was your ex-boyfriend **like**?	**He was** impatient.
What kind of people do you like?	**I like** generous **people.**

Talk 1

Discuss the questions with your partner.

1. Which of the words in Language Focus 1 describe your personality?
2. Can you think of any other words that describe your personality?

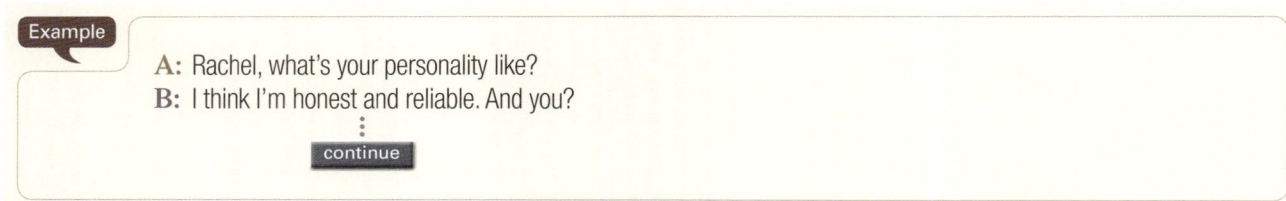

Example

A: Rachel, what's your personality like?
B: I think I'm honest and reliable. And you?

continue

Dialogue 2 *Listen to the dialogue and practice.*

Sue: It's strange. We both go to the same college, but we've never met before.
Mark: Yes, I know! What are you studying?
Sue: I'm studying English literature.
Mark: Oh, so your professor is Professor Smith, right?
Sue: Actually it's *Smyth*, not Smith. She's a brilliant woman, but she's a little cold. She's so serious all the time! Also, she can be cruel. My friend forgot her homework last week. Professor Smyth shouted at her in front of the whole class. She made her cry! Of course, she's very intelligent, but not so good with people.
Mark: She sounds like a difficult person. Luckily my professor, Professor Murray, is easygoing and charming! The girls all love him! He's always calm, and takes time to explain things that we don't understand. Also, he's very sociable. Sometimes he eats lunch with us. He is strict though. He makes sure we do our homework on time and doesn't accept any excuses. I think it's important for a professor to be strict. He's very hard-working, and he expects us to be the same.
Sue: And what about you? I know all about your professor now, but I don't know what *you* are like.
Mark: Well, I'm extremely romantic.
Sue: Oh really?! Well, you're certainly confident.

Comprehension Check!

1. How does Sue feel about her professor? Why?
2. Does Mark like his professor? Why?

Language Focus 2

Discussing Ideal Personalities

What do you think a professor **should be like?**	I think it's important for a professor to be strict, because he/she needs to control the students.
What kind of personality should a professor **have?**	A professor should be strict, so that he/she can control the students.

More Adjectives

She's a/an **brilliant/intelligent** woman.
Sometimes my boyfriend is too **cold/serious**.
I like **easygoing/calm** people.
The teacher is too **strict with/cruel to** the students.
People say I'm a **charming** guy, but they don't trust me.
I admire **hard-working** people.
It's easy to get along with **sociable** people.
My girlfriend used to be **romantic**, but she never tells me she loves me these days.
I have a lot of experience so I feel **confident**.

Pronunciation

Contrastive Stress

Discover Pronunciation!
Listen to the extracts from Dialogue 2.

Mark: Oh, so your professor is Professor Smith, right?
Sue: Actually it's **Smyth**, not Smith.

Sue: And what about you? I know all about your professor now, but I don't know what **you** are like.

We use contrastive stress to correct someone and to emphasize words.

Practice Pronunciation!
One word in the dialogues should be stressed. Underline the word, and then practice the dialogues with your partner.

❶ **A:** We agreed to meet at eight-thirty, didn't we?
   B: No, we agreed to meet at seven-thirty. You're so unreliable!

❷ **A:** Do you like your teacher?
   B: Well, I liked my old teacher, but my new teacher is very strict.

Talk 2

A Decide with your partner if the personality adjectives in the box are good or bad for a husband or wife. Give reasons for your decisions.

> **Example**: I think it's good for a husband to be faithful so that his wife can trust him. I think it's bad for a husband to be bad-tempered, because his wife couldn't get along with him.

adventurous	aggressive	ambitious	annoying	arrogant	artistic
bad-tempered	caring	cautious	cheerful	childish	competitive
determined	dynamic	emotional	energetic	entertaining	enthusiastic
faithful	gentle	irritating	passionate	picky	self-confident
sensitive	sophisticated	stingy	suspicious	witty	

B Work in two groups. Choose five words from this lesson to describe the perfect wife or husband. Then choose five words to describe a bad wife or husband. Order the words 1–5 in the spaces below, 1 being the most important, and 5 being the least important. Discuss and give reasons for your choices.

> **Example**:
> A: I think the most important thing for a wife is to be energetic.
> B: Why do you think that?
> continue

Perfect Wife/Husband	Bad Wife/Husband
❶	❶
❷	❷
❸	❸
❹	❹
❺	❺

Talk 3

A Think of words to describe the people's personalities with your partner.

> **Example:** Serena likes going out so she is outgoing and sociable.

BLIND DATE

 Serena	 Gonzalo	 Nicole	 Harry
• likes going out • enjoys meeting new people • reads long books about science **likes people who are:** patient, calm, positive	• enjoys relaxing in the park • often buys flowers for his girlfriends • sometimes feels sad about life **likes people who are:** smart, charming, hard-working	• works late until everything is done • likes buying dinner for her friends • doesn't like waiting for things **likes people who are:** easygoing, honest, generous	• doesn't like meeting new people • always speaks nicely to people but sometimes tells lies • gets along well with people **likes people who are:** intelligent, reliable, hard-working
 Sarah	 Peter	 Michelle	 Vincent
• often works late • regularly cancels appointments with friends • was the best student in her class **likes people who are:** romantic, calm, easygoing	• always tells the truth • buys expensive gifts • never gets angry **likes people who are:** sociable, generous, outgoing	• works as a scientist • has two jobs • always does what she says she will do **likes people who are:** shy, polite, patient	• usually feels happy about life • works as a middle school teacher • likes reading **likes people who are:** patient, outgoing, intelligent

B Talk with your partner to find the best blind date for the people in **A**.

> **Example:**
> **A:** Serena likes people who are calm.
> **B:** Then maybe she should date Gonzalo. He's calm. But he's also negative sometimes.
> **A:** Hmm … Serena likes people who are positive. Maybe someone else would be better.
> ⋮
> continue

i Read

A Read the posts from an internet dating forum. What is suzy10's question? What advice do the answers give?

Do opposites attract?

View previous topic   View next topic

Author	Message
suzy10	Posted: Thu Feb 24, 10:26 am I recently met a new guy. I really like him and we get along well, but we have opposite personalities. Should I continue with this relationship or forget about it?
john_k	Posted: Thu Feb 24, 13:39 pm People often say that opposites attract. Different personalities can be exciting at first, but what about the long term? For example, if you are outgoing and he is shy, how will you feel going to parties alone? Or, if you're romantic and he isn't, will you be happy when he doesn't organize anything special on your anniversary? A relationship with someone who has a different personality may seem a good idea at first, but over time you might change your mind.
whateva	Posted: Thu Feb 24, 15:47 pm A relationship between opposites can work if both people are open-minded and flexible. If you are stubborn, things will be very difficult. You need to communicate well and understand each other's differences.
Back to top	(new topic) (post reply)

B Discuss the questions with your partner.

1. Have you ever dated someone with a similar or different personality to your own? What was your experience?
2. Do you think that opposites attract? Why / Why not?
3. What advice would you give to suzy10?

i Write

Write a description of one of the people in the list.

1. an unforgettable teacher
2. your best friend
3. one of your classmates or co-workers
4. your girlfriend/boyfriend or wife/husband

Lesson 3 · 33

Lesson 4
Are you feeling OK?

Warm-Up

A How do the people feel? Match the feelings with the people.

| depressed | delighted | nervous | curious |
| angry | bored | embarrassed | exhausted |

B Talk with your partner about the last time you had the feelings in **A**.

Dialogue 1 — Listen to the dialogue and practice.

Simon: Hey, Jules. What's up?
Jules: Hi, Simon. I just got back from my business trip to Australia, so I'm feeling quite tired.
Simon: How did the trip go?
Jules: Pretty well. At first I was a little anxious because it was my first business trip. Also, I'd never been to Australia before. But everything went well. I made an important deal, so my manager is satisfied with me. So now I feel relieved.
Simon: Wow, I'm delighted to hear that. You must feel very proud. Anyway, I was disappointed that you couldn't come to my birthday party last week.
Jules: Yes, I'm really sorry I missed it. You're not angry with me, are you?
Simon: No, of course not! Just don't miss the next one!
Jules: OK, I won't. By the way, you don't look too good. In fact, you look exhausted. Are you feeling OK?
Simon: Actually I stayed up all night last night working on a report. I finally finished it though.
Jules: Great! Then take a rest today. You deserve it!

Comprehension Check!

1. How do Simon and Jules feel?
2. Why do they feel that way?

Language Focus 1

Talking About Feelings	
How do you feel?	**I feel** tired.
How are you feeling?	**I'm feeling** tired.
Are you OK?	Actually, **I'm** tired.
You look tired. What's up? / What's the matter?	I just came back from a business trip.
Why do you feel tired?	**Because I** just came back from a business trip.

Talk 1

A Match the sentence beginnings to the correct endings.

1. I'm **exhausted from**
2. I'm **anxious about**
3. I'm **relieved that**
4. I'm **curious about**
5. I'm **hopeful that**
6. I'm **confused about**
7. I'm **depressed about**
8. I'm **disappointed with**

a. the new restaurant. Let's try it sometime.
b. things will get better soon.
c. split**ting** up with my boyfriend.
d. my blind date.
e. my low test score.
f. work**ing** late all week.
g. my sister got home safely despite the bad weather.
h. some of the things we learned in class today.

B Roleplay conversations with your partner, using the beginnings of the sentences in **A**.

> **Example**
> **A:** You look confused. What's up?
> **B:** I'm confused about where to go on vacation next year.
> **A:** Really? Why?
> **B:** I can't decide whether to go to Italy or France.
> **A:** Well, how about visiting both?
> **B:** That sounds like a good idea.

Dialogue 2
Listen to the dialogue and practice.

Scott: Rita, are you OK? You look a little under the weather.
Rita: Oh, it's OK. I'm just exhausted from working on our new project.
Scott: I'm sorry to hear that. Yesterday you were in high spirits. What happened?
Rita: Our deadline changed so now we have a lot of work to finish this week.
Scott: Well, look on the bright side. By the end of the week, the work will be finished. Why don't you go outside and take a walk for 30 minutes. Or how about going to the swimming pool after work? That always makes me feel better.
Rita: Yes, that's a good idea. I'm just in a bad mood today, that's all.
Scott: Sure! You'll soon be on form again. Keep your chin up!

Comprehension Check!

1. How does Rita feel? Why?
2. What does Scott say to cheer Rita up?
3. What does Scott suggest doing?

Language Focus 2

Fixed Expressions for Feelings	
Positive	**Negative**
You seem to be **in high spirits** today. [happy]	I'm **in a bad mood** today. [unhappy]
I'm feeling really **on form** this week. [good]	You look a little **under the weather.** [unwell]

Pronunciation

Compound Nouns

Discover Pronunciation!
Listen to the extracts from Dialogue 1 and Dialogue 2. Notice the stress in the compound nouns.

Jules: Hi, Simon. I just got back from my **business trip** to Australia, so I'm feeling quite tired.

Scott: Or how about going to the **swimming pool** after work?

Scott: I'm sorry to hear that. Yesterday you were in **high spirits**. What happened?

In most compound nouns, the stress is on the first part of the compound noun (<u>business</u> trip, <u>swimming</u> pool). In some compound nouns that are adjective + noun, both parts are stressed (<u>high</u> <u>spirits</u>).

Practice Pronunciation!
Practice asking and answering the questions with your partner.

① Do you like going to **swimming pools**?

② When did you last go to a **bookstore**? Did you buy anything there?

③ Do you like **fast food**?

④ When were you last in **high spirits**? What made you feel that way?

Talk 2

Talk with your partner about how you feel in each situation.

> **Example**
> **A:** How do you feel when it's a rainy day?
> **B:** I'm often in a bad mood on rainy days. What about you?
> **A:** I feel delighted because I love rainy days.

1. When it's your birthday.
2. When you're on vacation.
3. When your cell phone stops working.
4. When it's the first day of school.
5. When it's a sunny/rainy day.
6. When you have a blind date.

Language Focus 3

Making Suggestions

Why don't you take a break?
What about tak**ing** a walk?
I suggest that you spend some time with your friends.
If I was you, I'd get some sleep.

Cheering People Up

Look on the bright side. It will soon be the weekend.
Keep your chin up.
Everything will be OK.
Don't worry about it.
Relax.
Things aren't so bad.

Talk 3

A Decide with your partner what the causes of the people's feelings are. Then make suggestions to make the people feel better.

Cause	Feeling	Suggestions
studying for an important exam	 stressed	• take a break sometimes • do some exercise or play a sport
	 exhausted	
	 in a bad mood	
	 bored	
	 under the weather	

B Roleplay conversations with a different partner, using the information in **A**. Try to cheer your partner up.

Example
A: You look stressed. What's the matter?
B: I've been studying for an important exam so I haven't been sleeping much.
A: Don't worry about it. And why don't you take a break? If I was you, I'd do some exercise.
B: That's a good idea.
A: Yes. Keep your chin up.

i Read

A Read the descriptions of people's embarrassing moments. Why did the people feel embarrassed?

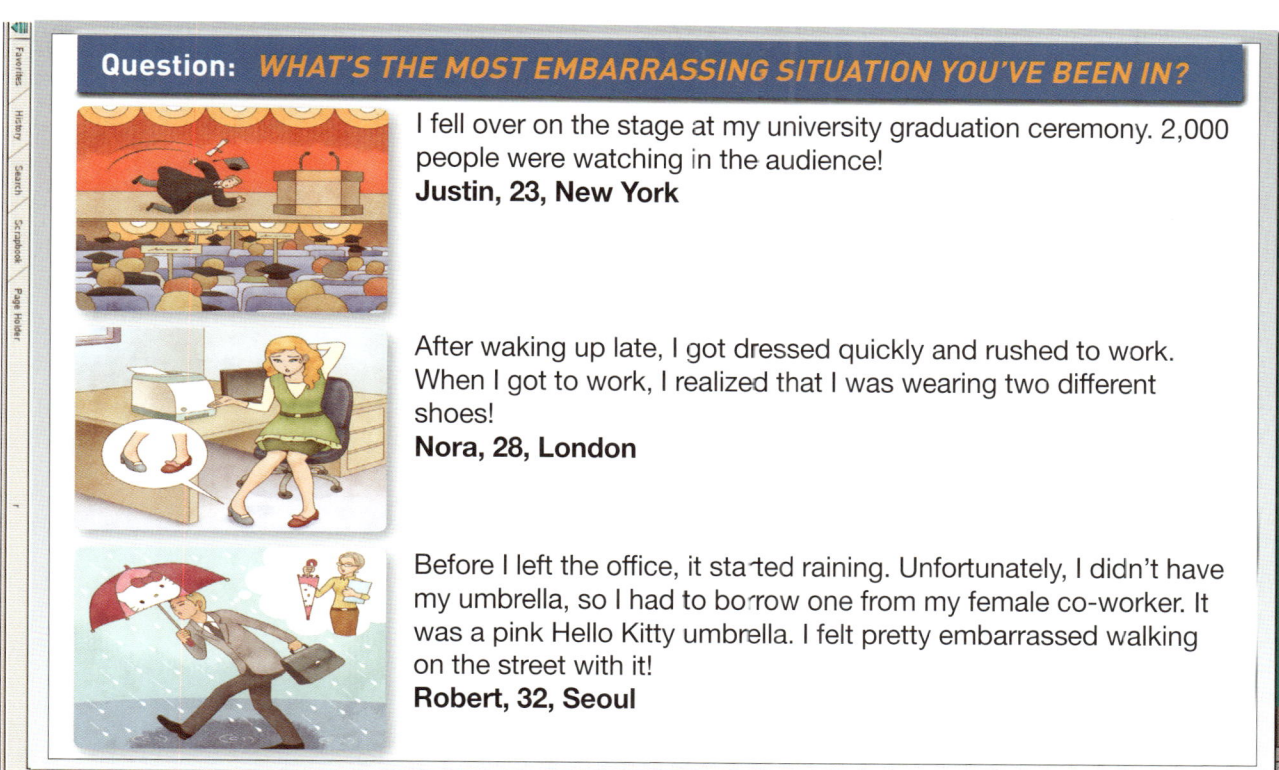

Question: WHAT'S THE MOST EMBARRASSING SITUATION YOU'VE BEEN IN?

I fell over on the stage at my university graduation ceremony. 2,000 people were watching in the audience!
Justin, 23, New York

After waking up late, I got dressed quickly and rushed to work. When I got to work, I realized that I was wearing two different shoes!
Nora, 28, London

Before I left the office, it started raining. Unfortunately, I didn't have my umbrella, so I had to borrow one from my female co-worker. It was a pink Hello Kitty umbrella. I felt pretty embarrassed walking on the street with it!
Robert, 32, Seoul

B Discuss the questions with your partner.
1. Which situation do you think is the most embarrassing?
2. Have you had the same or similar experiences? Tell your partner what happened and how you felt.
3. What is the most embarrassing situation you've been in? Tell your partner about it.
4. Tell the rest of the class your partner's story.

i Write

When you feel bad, what do you do to cheer yourself up? Choose one of the feelings below and write about what you do to make yourself feel better.

| in a bad mood | under the weather | stressed | exhausted | bored | angry | anxious |

Example
When I'm stressed, I lie down in a dark room and try to relax. Sometimes I play some soft music to help me calm down. Then, I think calmly of solutions to my problem. If possible, I plan how to fix the problem. That way, I feel much better.

Lesson 5: Why don't you go see a doctor?

Warm-Up

A Complete the sentences using the appropriate words from the box.

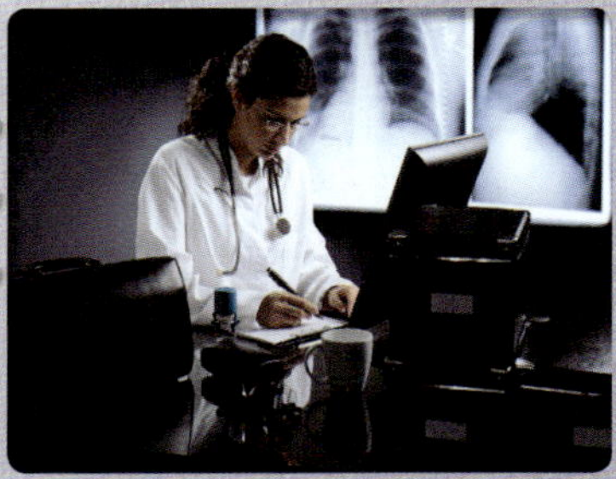

A: I have a rash. Where should I go?
B: You should see a/an _____.

A: I have a stomachache. Where should I go?
B: You should see a/an _____.

A: I want a nose job. Where should I go?
B: You should see a/an _____.

A: My child is sick. What should I do?
B: Why don't you take your child to see a/an _____?

A: I have a sore throat. What should I do?
B: Why don't you see a/an _____?

A: I'm having a baby. What should I do?
B: Why don't you see a/an _____?

| dermatologist | ENT doctor | obstetrician |
| pediatrician | physician | plastic surgeon |

B Discuss the questions with your partner.

1. Have you ever given advice to someone who was sick? What did you advise the person to do?
2. What is the best advice that someone has given you? Tell your partner about it.

Dialogue 1 — Listen to the dialogue and practice.

Anna: Hi, Lisa. It's Anna.
Lisa: Hi, Anna. What's up? You don't sound well. Are you sick or something?
Anna: Yes, I feel very sick. I think I'm coming down with a cold.
Lisa: Really? What are your symptoms?
Anna: I have a headache and a sore throat. Also, I have an earache, and I'm coughing. I feel terrible.
Lisa: It sounds like you do have a cold. You should take a day off and rest tomorrow.
Anna: I think so, too. I'll call in sick tomorrow first thing in the morning.
Lisa: Yes, I think you should. Why don't you go see a doctor as well? You'd better call the doctor's office and make an appointment.
Anna: Yes, I will. Hopefully I can see him sometime in the morning.
Lisa: OK. Until then, I suggest you drink lots of water and stay in bed. Get plenty of rest.
Anna: That's a good idea. Thanks for the advice.

Comprehension Check!

1. What are Anna's symptoms?
2. What is she going to do tomorrow?
3. What is Lisa's suggestion?

Language Focus 1

Giving Advice 1
You should take a day off and rest.
You should stay in bed.
I suggest you drink lots of water.
Why don't you go see a doctor?
You'd better make an appointment.

Talk 1

Complete the table, using the words from the box.

Type of Doctor	Specialization
	development and diseases of children
	general medicine
	problems of the brain and nerves
	pregnancy and birth
	surgery to change people's appearance
	skin problems
	ear, nose, and throat problems
	teeth and dental problems

dentist	dermatologist	ENT doctor
neurologist	obstetrician	pediatrician
physician	plastic surgeon	

Dialogue 2 — Listen to the dialogue and practice.

Julie: How are you doing, Mike? You don't seem too happy this morning. What's the matter?
Mike: Well, I guess it's because I didn't get much sleep last night. I went to bed early but woke up a lot. When that happens, I feel really tired.
Julie: That's too bad. When people have trouble sleeping, they don't feel refreshed when they wake up. Some people even feel depressed and irritable.
Mike: Exactly. Whenever I don't sleep properly, I feel sleepy throughout the day. I sometimes fall asleep during classes and presentations. I have trouble paying attention and focusing on tasks.
Julie: Let me suggest a few things that might help. First of all, reduce your stress. Do something that relaxes you. Next, avoid alcohol and caffeine. Also, eat only light food before you go to bed.
Mike: Maybe I should try that. But if that still doesn't work, then what should I do?
Julie: In that case, I think you should see a doctor. You'd better find out what the problem is.
Mike: All right, that sounds good to me. I'll take your advice. Thank you so much.
Julie: My pleasure, Mike. You need to take care of yourself. See you later!

Comprehension Check!

1. What is the matter with Mike?
2. What is Julie's advice?

Language Focus 2

Giving Advice 2
Let me suggest a few things that might help.
I think you should see a doctor.
You need to take care of yourself.
Avoid alcohol and caffeine.
Thank you. I'll take your advice.

 Talk 2

A Listen to the dialogue. What does the first speaker want to know? What advice does the second speaker give?

> **Q:** I want to go to college in the US. What does it take to get accepted to good colleges there?
> **A:** Good colleges look for strong academic records, extracurricular activities, and good letters of recommendation.
> **Q:** Do I need to take a test?
> **A:** Colleges have different test requirements. You may or may not have to take the SAT. Most colleges require international students to submit a score from an English language test.
> **Q:** When should I start planning for applying to college?
> **A:** I advise you to start planning about two years in advance. Apply to colleges about a year before the course starts.

B Discuss the questions with your partner.

① Would you like to go to college in the US? Why/Why not?
② Imagine that your partner wants to improve his/her English to go to a college abroad. What advice would you give him/her?

Pronunciation

Vowel Sounds /ɪ/ and /iː/

Discover Pronunciation!
Listen to the extracts from Dialogue 1 and Dialogue 2. Practice saying the underlined words.

Lisa: Hi, Anna. What's up? You don't sound well. Are you <u>sick</u> or something?
Anna: Yes, I <u>feel</u> very <u>sick</u>. I <u>think</u> I'm coming down with a cold.

Julie: Some people even <u>feel</u> depressed and irritable.
Mike: Exactly. Whenever I don't <u>sleep</u> properly, I <u>feel</u> <u>sleepy</u> throughout the day. I sometimes fall <u>asleep</u> during classes and presentations.

Practice Pronunciation!
A Listen to the words and practice saying them.

/ɪ/	six sick chickens	in the middle	a slippery hill	hit it
/iː/	feel sleepy	a deep sleep	please keep it	seek peace

B Say ONE word from each pair to your partner. Does your partner know which word you said?

	/iː/	/ɪ/
❶	bean	bin
❷	sheep	ship
❸	leave	live
❹	seat	sit

Talk 3

A Read the travel advice. Which piece of advice do you think is the most useful?

1. **Pack light and travel light.** You will walk a lot in Europe, so don't take heavy luggage.
2. **Wear good hiking shoes and socks.** You need good arch support.
3. **Bring a wash cloth.** European hotels usually don't provide them.
4. **Learn some foreign words and phrases.** Not everybody speaks English!
5. **Book hotels in advance.** It's very difficult to find rooms during high season.
6. **Plan your meals carefully to save money.** Buy food at grocery stores.
7. **Rent a car.** It can be cheaper than public transportation if two or more people are traveling. A car can also make it easier to get around.

B Discuss the questions with your partner.

1. Advise your partner on what to take in his/her suitcase to Europe. Give reasons for your advice.
2. Imagine that you and your partner are going to visit Europe for ten days. Discuss where to go and what to eat.

i Read

A Read the question and answer from an online health magazine. What is the question and what advice is given?

Q:
Dear Doctor,
For the past few weeks, I haven't been able to get much sleep. I often become very anxious before going to bed. I have a hard time falling asleep, and even if I fall asleep, I wake up a lot during the night. Is there a natural way I can sleep well? I really want to have a good night's sleep.

Sleepless in Seattle

A:
Dear Sleepless,
Insomnia is an inability to fall asleep or stay asleep. In other words, it is sleeplessness. It can last anywhere from one night to a few weeks or even longer. When people want to sleep but can't, they wind up feeling more tired, cranky, and even depressed. The following tips are intended to help you avoid insomnia and sleep through the night:

- ☑ Don't overeat in the evening.
- ☑ Avoid drinking too much fluid prior to bedtime.
- ☑ Avoid alcohol and caffeine.
- ☑ Avoid taking naps during the day, especially in the afternoon.
- ☑ Reduce your stress levels. Do something that relaxes you.
- ☑ Exercise regularly during the day.
- ☑ Keep your bedroom clean and create a quiet and peaceful environment.

B Discuss the questions with your partner.
1. Have you ever had difficulty sleeping? If so, how did you feel?
2. What do you think caused your insomnia? What did you do about it?
3. What advice would you give to people who are having trouble sleeping?

i Write

A Write a question to an online doctor to ask for advice about a health problem.

B Write a reply to your friend's text message to give him/her advice.

I'm really sick. Headache, runny nose … I think I have a temperature, too. ☹ What am I gonna do???

Lesson 6

People say it's the best in the world.

Warm-Up

 Match the words with the pictures.

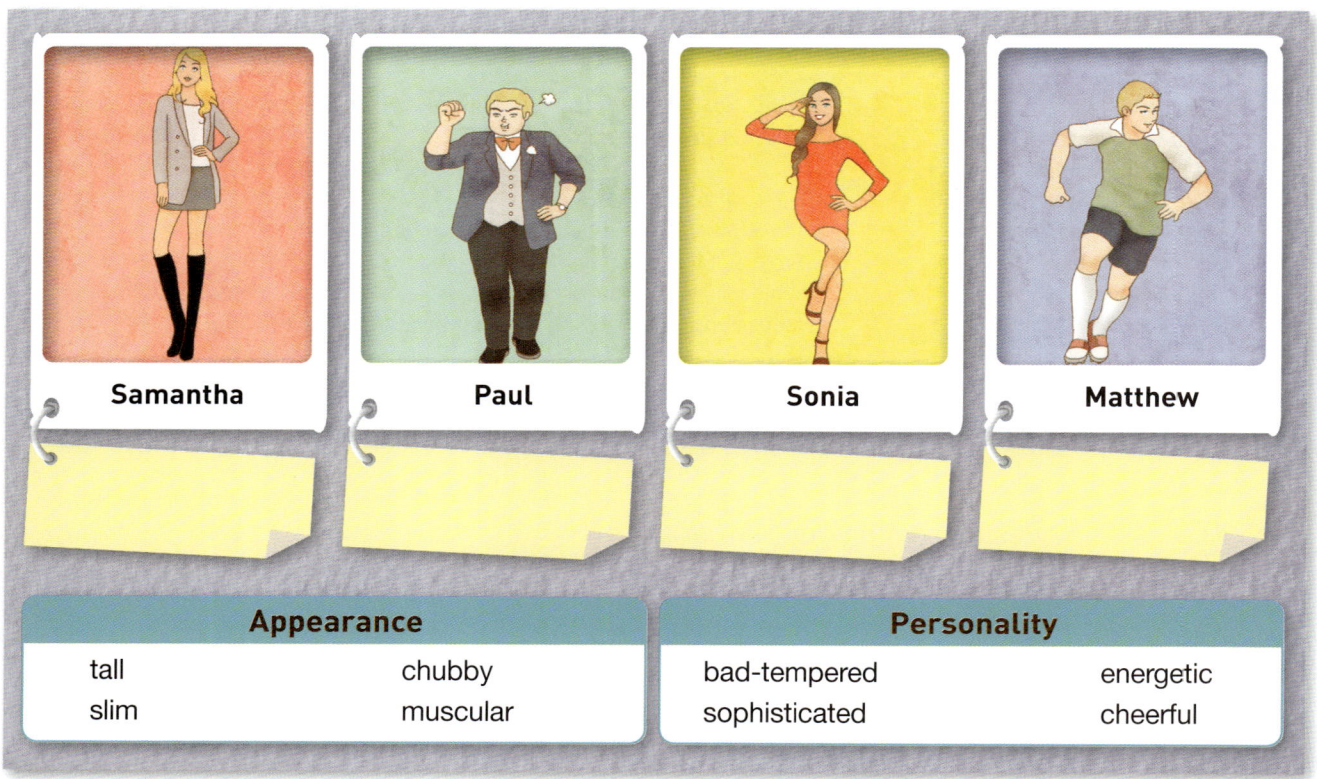

Appearance		Personality	
tall	chubby	bad-tempered	energetic
slim	muscular	sophisticated	cheerful

B Complete the sentences, referring to the pictures in **A**.

① **Q:** Who is taller: Paul or Sonia?
   A: _____ is _____ than _____.

② **Q:** Who is chubbier: Matthew or Paul?
   A: _____ is _____ _____ than _____.

③ **Q:** Who looks more cheerful: Sonia or Samantha?
   A: _____ looks _____ _____ than _____.

④ **Q:** _____?
   A: _____.

⑤ **Q:** _____?
   A: _____.

Dialogue 1 — Listen to the dialogue and practice.

Frank: Jessica, have you decided yet who we're going to hire to be the new receptionist?
Jessica: I haven't made a final decision yet. According to their resumes, all four candidates are well-qualified. Who do you think is the most suitable for the position?
Frank: Well, I think Hannah seems more reliable than the other three candidates. Hannah worked at the same company for three years, but the others changed jobs quite often. She also seems smarter than the others.
Jessica: You're right. Also, I thought Hannah was the most positive and outgoing of the four candidates during the interview.
Frank: Yes, I agree with you. So, are you going to offer her the job?
Jessica: Probably. I'll take one last look through the resumes this afternoon and then make a decision.

Comprehension Check!

1. Who is Hannah?
2. What do Frank and Jessica think about her?

Language Focus

Comparing Things

Who is smart**er**, Tony **or** Annie?	Tony **is** smart**er than** Annie.
Is Tony smart**er than** Annie?	**No**, Annie **is as** smart **as** Tony.
Who is less smart, Tony **or** Annie?	Annie **is less** smart **than** Tony.
Who is more positive?	Annie **is more** positive **than** Tony.
Who is less positive?	Tony **is less** positive **than** Annie.
Who is better?	**I think** Annie **is** better **than** Tony.
Who is worse?	Tony **is** worse **than** Annie.
Who is the smart**est**?	Tony **is the** smart**est**.
Who is the least smart?	Annie **is the least** smart.
Who is the most positive?	Annie **is the most** positive.
Who is the least positive?	Tony **is the least** positive.
Who is the best?	**I think** Annie **is the** best.
Who is the worst?	**I think** Tony **is the** worst.

Pronunciation

Word Stress With -er and -est

Discover Pronunciation!
Listen to the words and notice the way the speakers stress different syllables.

smart	old	young	busy
smarter	older	younger	busier
smartest	oldest	youngest	busiest

For words ending in *-er* and *-est*, the stress stays on the same syllable.

Practice Pronunciation!
Practice saying the words above with your partner.

Talk 1

A Decide with your partner who in your class best matches the descriptions below. Write their names.

Example

A: Who is the most hard-working person in our class?
B: Let me think. James always does extra homework, so I think he is the most hard-working.
A: I think Joan is more hard-working than James. She has two jobs.
B: Yes, you're right. Joan is the most hard-working.

The Youngest Person	
The Oldest Person	
The Busiest Person	
The Most Hard-Working Person	
The Most Entertaining Person	
The Most Energetic Person	
The Most Cheerful Person	
The Most Stylish Person	

B Tell the class what you decided in **A**. Explain the reasons for your decisions.

Dialogue 2
Listen to the dialogue and practice.

Crystal: I'm planning to take a trip in the summer, but I can't decide where to go.
Robert: Oh, really? Where do you have in mind?
Crystal: I have two places in mind: Italy and France. Which country do you think is better?
Robert: As far as I'm concerned, Italy is better than France. There are lots of places to visit there. Also, I feel that Italy is more beautiful than France.
Crystal: Yes, I heard that, too. But what about French food? People say it's the best in the world.
Robert: Hmm … I don't agree. I'd say Italian food is better than French food. French cooking uses a lot of butter and cream, whereas Italian cooking is lighter and healthier.
Crystal: But I really want to see the Eiffel Tower. Do you think I could visit both countries?
Robert: Yes, why not? It's easy to travel between Italy and France by train or airplane.
Crystal: OK, I'll consider doing that then.

Comprehension Check!

❶ What is Crystal's problem?
❷ What does Robert suggest? Why?

Language Focus 2

Asking for and Giving Opinions	
Which country **do you think** is better?	**As far as I'm concerned,** Italy is the perfect place for a vacation.
Do you think Italy is **as** beautiful **as** France?	Yes, **I feel that** Italy is **as** beautiful **as** France.
Do you think I could visit both countries?	Yes, why not?
Don't you think French food is the best?	I don't agree. **I'd say** Italian food is better than French food.

Talk 2

Decide with your partner which one from each pair is better. Give reasons for your decisions.

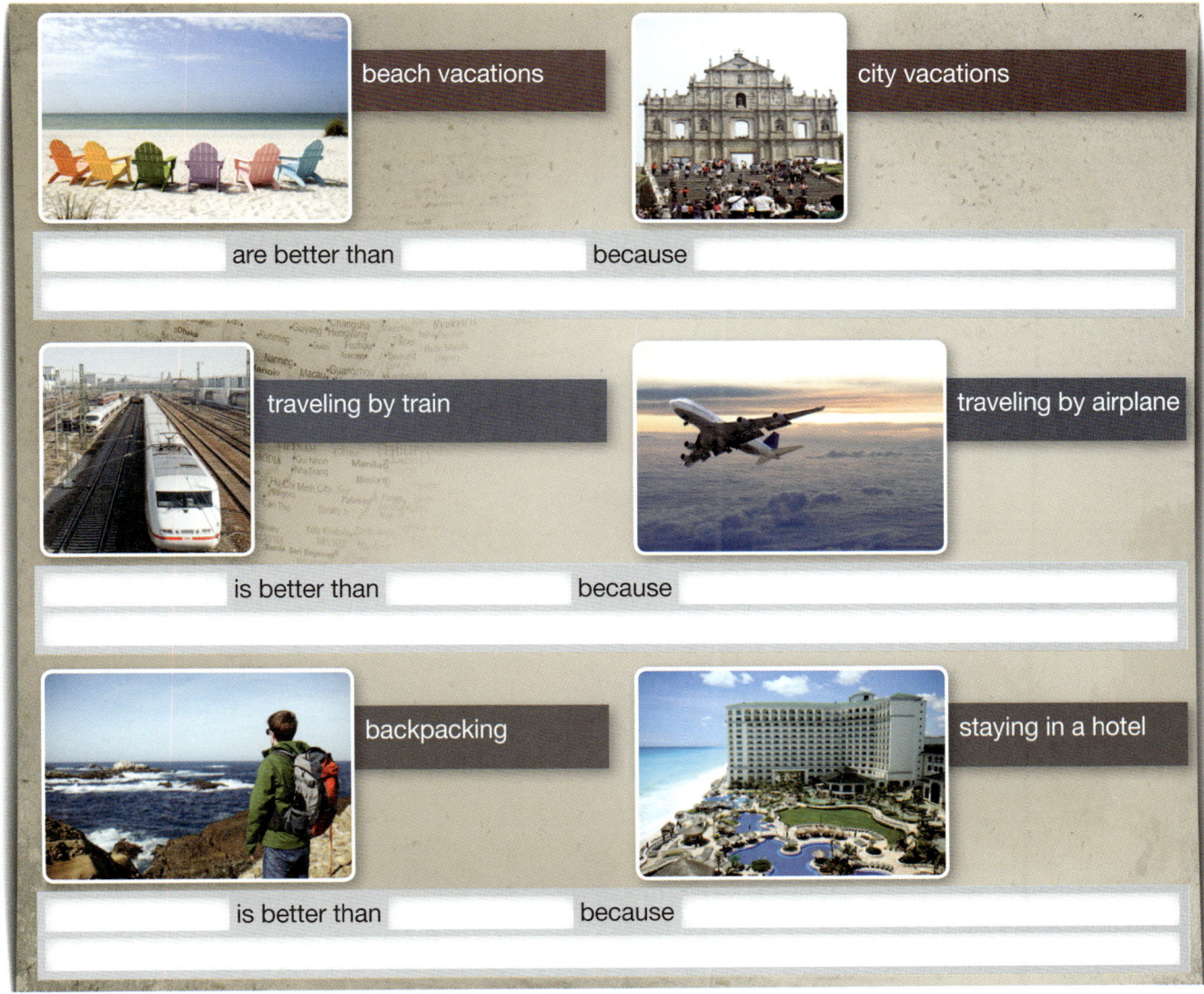

Talk 3

A Work in groups. Decide which of the vacation packages is the best. Give reasons for your decision.

Example

A: Which package do you think is better?
B: I feel that Package B is the best. It is cheaper than Package A.
A: But Package C is cheaper than Package B. Also, it is more popular with customers.
B: But don't you think that hotel is too far from the city center? The other hotels are closer.

continue

✤ Package A — Price: €2,200

- Hotel De Marco, Rome
- Distance from city center: 0.1 km
- Customer rating: 8/10
- Star rating: ★★★★★

- Includes: flight tickets ✓
  airport transfer ✗
  breakfast ✓
  dinner ✓
  free museum entry ✗
  free city bus tour ✓

✤ Package B — Price: €1,500

- Hotel Principessa, Rome
- Distance from city center: 2 km
- Customer rating: 5/10
- Star rating: ★★★

- Includes: flight tickets ✓
  airport transfer ✓
  breakfast ✓
  dinner ✓
  free museum entry ✓
  free city bus tour ✓

✤ Package C — Price: €1,200

- Hotel Lazio, Rome
- Distance from city center: 4 km
- Customer rating: 7/10
- Star rating: ★★

- Includes: flight tickets ✓
  airport transfer ✗
  breakfast ✗
  dinner ✗
  free museum entry ✓
  free city bus tour ✓

B Tell the class what you decided in **A**. Explain the reasons for your decision.

Example

We think Package C is the best because it's the cheapest.

continue

i Read

A Read the magazine article. Is the writer happy that she decided to travel overseas?

WANT TO CHANGE YOUR LIFE? TRAVEL!

Travel changed my life. Five years ago, I was a junior in college. I was shy and unconfident. Then, I spent a semester studying abroad in New Zealand. In New Zealand, I changed in many ways. Living independently in a foreign country made me feel more confident. I met people from many different countries and became more sociable and open-minded. During my vacation, I traveled around New Zealand and also visited Australia. This made me a more confident person. I'm so happy that I had the chance to live abroad, as it made me a better person. In fact, I'd say it was a life-changing experience.

B Discuss the questions with your partner.

1. What does the writer think about living abroad?
2. What was the writer like before she lived abroad?
3. What is the writer like now? What caused her to change?
4. Have you had any life-changing experiences? Describe what happened and how you changed.

i Write

Write a short magazine article in response to one of the questions.

1. What were you like five years ago? What has changed? What caused you to change?
2. Describe a life-changing experience. What happened? In what ways did you change?

Lesson 7

You look gorgeous in those skinny jeans.

Warm-Up

A Decide with your partner which THREE of the tips are the most important for a healthy life. Give reasons for your decisions.

Healthy Living Tips

- Exercise regularly.
- Get lots of rest. 
- Go to bed before 10 pm. 
- Work regular hours. 
- Reduce stress. 
- Drink more than two liters of water a day. 
- Eat fruits and vegetables. 
- Take vitamin pills. 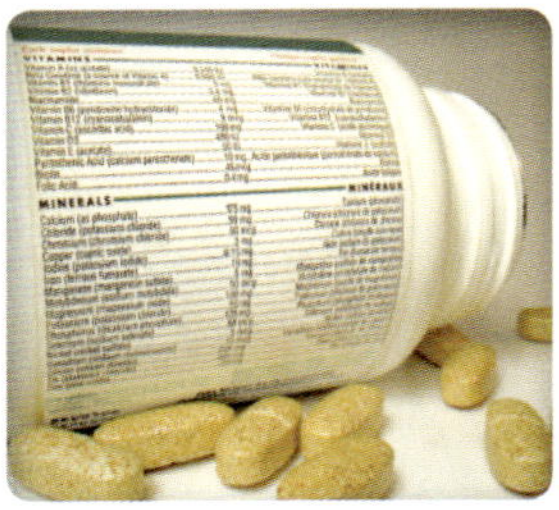

B Discuss the questions with your partner.

1. Do you follow any of the tips in **A**?
2. Which tips would you like to follow more?

Dialogue 1 *Listen to the dialogue and practice.*

John: Hello there! You look gorgeous in those skinny jeans. Have you lost some weight lately?
Kate: Yeah, I've been on a diet for a while. I went down a pants size so far.
John: Wow, that's great! So, what kind of diet are you on?
Kate: Well, I gave up junk food. Instead, I eat fruits and vegetables.
John: You don't mean that's all you eat, do you? Do you eat anything else?
Kate: Sure. I eat grilled chicken breast, fish, and tofu.
John: Sounds like you have a well-balanced meal plan. Do you also exercise?
Kate: Of course I do. I go for a walk every other day at the park near my home.
John: How much time do you spend walking when you go there?
Kate: I walk for about 40 minutes. After exercising, I feel so refreshed.
John: Good for you. I think I should start doing something to get in shape, too.

Comprehension Check!

1. What did Kate do to lose weight?
2. What does John think he should do?

Language Focus 1

Staying in Shape

She **is on a** low-carb **diet**.
I need to **lose weight**.
What do you do to **stay in shape**?
What did you do to **get in shape**?
I gave up junk food.

Pronunciation

Sentence Stress

Discover Pronunciation!
Listen to the extract from Dialogue 1. Notice how the speaker stresses some words more than other words.

You look gorgeous in those skinny jeans. Have you lost some weight lately?

We stress important words (main verbs, nouns, adverbs, etc.) more than less important words (articles, auxiliary verbs, prepositions, pronouns, etc.).

Practice Pronunciation!
The important words in the sentences should be stressed. Underline the important words, and then practice the sentences with your partner.

1. I need to lose some weight.
2. I have been on a diet for three weeks.
3. Instead, I eat fruits and vegetables.
4. I walk for about 40 minutes.

Talk 1

Write the tips in the correct categories. Discuss and give reasons for your choices.

Dos and Don'ts of Healthy Weight Loss

Do ...	Don't ...
• exercise regularly	• starve yourself

- eat pizza
- have light dinners
- starve yourself ✓
- eat when you're not hungry
- eat lots of saturated fat
- eat salad/vegetables
- take multi-vitamins and minerals
- get enough sleep
- skip meals
- drink lots of water
- cut down on sodium
- overload on sweets
- eat French fries
- avoid all-you-can-eat buffets
- exercise regularly ✓
- drink soda

Lesson 7 · 61

Dialogue 2
Listen to the dialogue and practice.

Jason: Hi, Sarah. Did you watch *Diet Champs* last night? It was so amazing!
Sarah: Oh, yes! I couldn't miss it! It's my favorite show.
Jason: What did you think of the winner? She lost 43 kg in 12 weeks!
Sarah: Yeah, incredible! Did you see her 'before' and 'after' pictures? She looked so different!
Jason: Yeah. She must have worked really hard. I tried to lose weight recently, but I failed.
Sarah: Did you know men lose weight faster than women?
Jason: No, I didn't. Why's that?
Sarah: First of all, men have more muscle so they can burn calories more quickly.
Jason: Oh, I see!
Sarah: Also, women tend to store fat. So they have to work harder to lose weight.
Jason: Wow, how interesting! I feel like working out now. I'd better go to the gym!
Sarah: That's a great idea.

Comprehension Check!
❶ What does Sarah say about men and women?
❷ What does Jason decide to do?

Language Focus 2

Losing Weight	
She lost 43 **kg in** 12 weeks!	She must have **worked really hard**.
Men **lose weight** faster than women.	Women tend to **store fat**.
I feel like **working out** now.	

Talk 2

Discuss the questions with your partner, using the information in Talk 1.

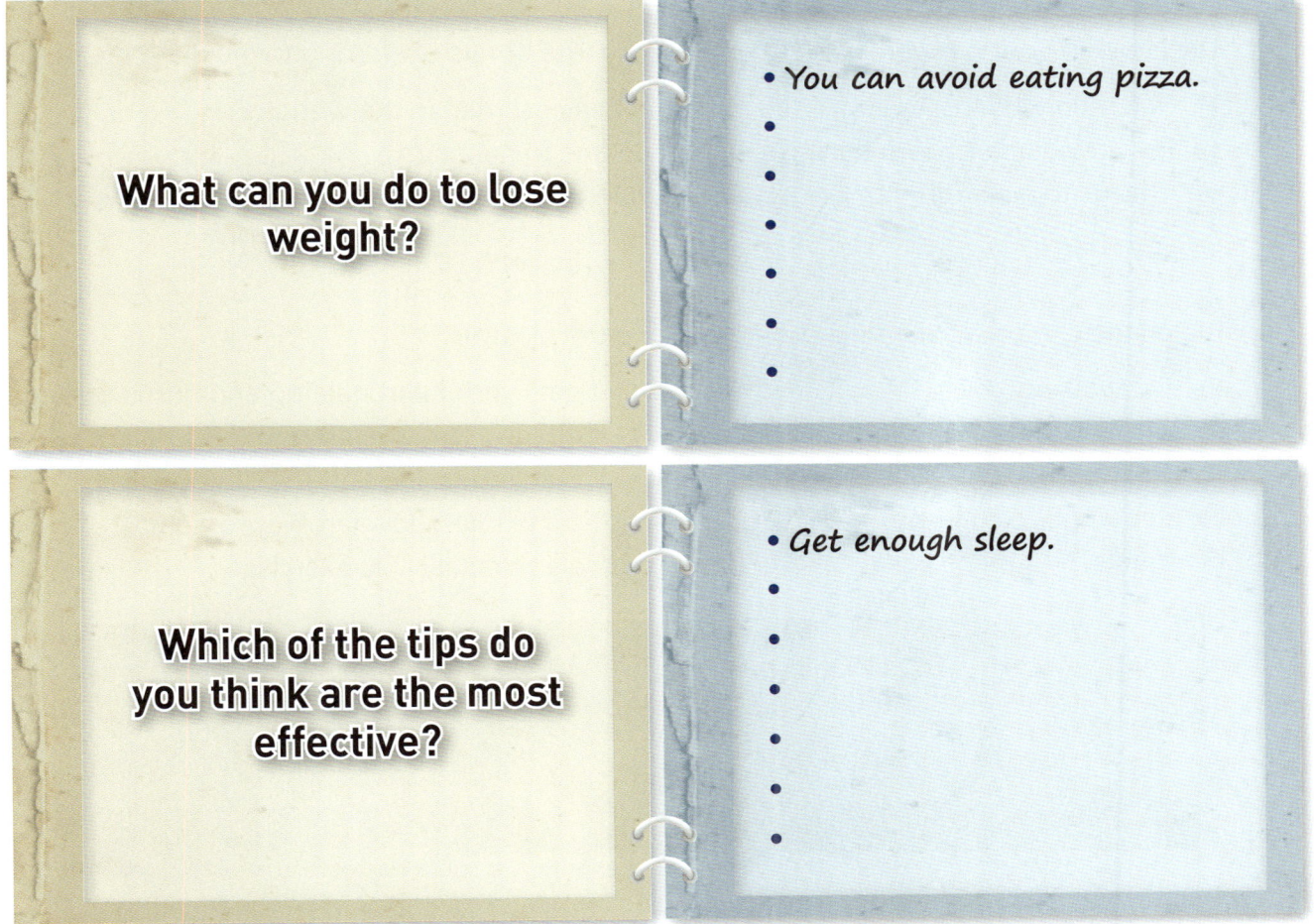

What can you do to lose weight?

- You can avoid eating pizza.
-
-
-
-
-
-

Which of the tips do you think are the most effective?

- Get enough sleep.
-
-
-
-
-
-

Talk 3

A Practice the dialogue with your partner.

A: Hey, did you hear the story about the man who lost 250 kg?
B: No. How much did he weigh before he lost that much weight?
A: He used to weigh 560 kg. He was in the *Guinness Book of Records*. He was so huge that he couldn't leave his room!
B: Wow! But what made him lose so much weight?
A: Well, he decided to marry his girlfriend. She encouraged and supported him to lose weight.
B: Amazing! That's the power of love!

B Decide with your partner if the statements are true or false, referring to the dialogue in **A**.

1. The man who lost weight used to be the heaviest man in the world.
2. He stayed in his room because he had no one to help him.
3. Thanks to his girlfriend, he decided to change his life.

C Match the exercises with the descriptions and the pictures.

1. fast walking
2. jumping jacks
3. push-ups
4. stepping
5. squats

a. It gets your heart beating and burns calories.
b. It builds your arm strength.
c. It builds your leg and buttock muscles
d. It's a whole-body aerobic workout.
e. It's a great aerobic exercise.

i Read

Complete the questionnaire for your partner by asking him/her the questions. Circle the appropriate answers. Then add up the score to find out how fit your partner is.

How healthy are you?

1. How often do you exercise?
   a. once a week
   b. 2–3 times a week
   c. every day

2. How often do you eat fruits and vegetables?
   a. 1–2 times a week
   b. 3–4 times a week
   c. every day

3. How many hours do you sleep at night?
   a. 5 or fewer
   b. 8–12 hours
   c. 6–8 hours

4. How many cigarettes do you smoke per day?
   a. more than 10
   b. less than 10
   c. none

5. How often do you feel stressed?
   a. every day
   b. every week
   c. rarely

Key	a = 0 points	b = 1 point	c = 2 points
9–10: Excellent	You are very fit and healthy!		
7–8: Good	You are healthy at the moment, but try a little harder to get in shape.		
5–6: Average	You should start thinking more about your health. Try harder to stay in shape.		
0–4: Poor	Warning! You should start taking care of yourself asap! Eat properly and do some exercise.		

i Write

Write about how healthy you are. Refer to the fitness questionnaire in i Read for ideas.

Lesson 8
Do you do a lot of exercise?

Warm-Up

A Talk with your partner about how often you do each activity.

B Discuss the questions with your partner.
1. How healthy are the activities in **A**?
2. Do you think you should do each activity more or less often?

Dialogue 1 Listen to the dialogue and practice.

John: Thanks for being with us on the show today, Sharon.
Sharon: You're welcome, John. It's great to be here. I've always wanted to be on your show.
John: Thanks. Now, we all know that you're married, you're in your forties, and you have three kids. Yet, you're in fantastic shape. What's your secret? Do you do a lot of exercise?
Sharon: Yes, I often go to the gym.
John: Oh, really? How often?
Sharon: I go every other day, except when I'm too busy filming my TV show.
John: How much time do you spend working out at the gym?
Sharon: I spend around one and a half hours working out. Then I usually go to the sauna to relax for a while before going home.
John: Well, your fitness routine certainly seems to work well.

Comprehension Check!

1. What does Sharon do to stay in shape?
2. What most likely is Sharon's job?

Language Focus

Talking About Frequency

Do you (ever) go to the gym?	I **always** go to the gym. **almost always** **usually** **regularly** **often** **sometimes** **occasionally** **seldom** **rarely** **hardly ever** **never**
How often do you go to the gym? **Do you often** go to the gym?	I go to the gym **every other day**. **every Sunday**. **once / twice / three times a week**. I **don't** go to the gym **very often**.
How much time do you spend work**ing** out at the gym?	**I spend** one and a half hours (work**ing** out) at the gym.

 Pronunciation

Sentence Stress

Discover Pronunciation!
Listen to the extract from Dialogue 1. Notice how the speaker stresses some words more than other words.

● • ● • ● • ● • ● • ●
Thanks for being with us on the show today, Sharon.

Remember to stress important words (main verbs, nouns, adverbs, etc.) more than less important words (articles, auxiliary verbs, prepositions, pronouns, etc.).

Practice Pronunciation!
Match the sentences with the stress patterns. Then practice the sentences with your partner.

1. It's great to be here.
2. Yes, I often go to the gym.
3. How often do you go there?
4. I go every other day.

a. ● • ● • ● • ● • ●
b. ● • ● • ● •
c. ● • ● • ● • ●
d. ● • ● • ● •

Talk 1

Sharon and her husband, Carl, both like to stay in shape. Write sentences about them, referring to the pictures.

Dialogue 2 — Listen to the dialogue and practice.

Jason: Hi, Denise. Welcome back! How was your trip to France?
Denise: It was great, thanks. I learned a lot about French culture.
Jason: Oh, really? Like what?
Denise: Well, French people seem to eat so much. Plus, they eat a lot more butter and cheese than Americans do. The food is quite rich.
Jason: Wow, I didn't know that. So, are French people fat?
Denise: Amazingly, they aren't fat! French people suffer less from obesity than Americans do.
Jason: How can that be?
Denise: I think it's because French people usually end their meals with a simple piece of fresh fruit. They don't regularly eat large desserts and ice cream like Americans do.
Jason: How about drinks though? Don't French people drink a lot of wine?
Denise: No, they almost always have just one glass of wine with their meals. Also, they rarely drink soft drinks like cola. They usually drink water.
Jason: That sounds like a more healthy way to eat and drink. Maybe I should go on a French diet!

Comprehension Check!

1. Where has Denise been?
2. What did she notice in the country she visited?

Talk 2

A Ask three classmates about their diets. Talk about the things in Talk 1, and two other things. Write the answers.

> Example
>
> **A:** How often do you eat fish?
> **B:** I eat fish twice a week.

B Tell the class what you found out about your classmates.

> Example
>
> I found out that Bradley eats fish twice a week. Rachel, on the other hand, eats fish only once a week.

Talk 3

Discuss the questions with your partner.

1. Have you ever been to a foreign country? What was the food like there? How healthy do you think it was?
2. If you haven't visited a foreign country, what do you know about food in other countries?

> Example
>
> **A:** Tina, have you ever been to a foreign country?
> **B:** Yes, I've been to Japan.
> **A:** What was the food like there?
> **B:** It was really healthy. People in Japan eat a lot of fish.
>
> continue

i Read

 Read the article from a health magazine. What is the Mediterranean diet?

■■ The World's Healthiest Diet?

Many doctors believe that the Mediterranean diet is the best in the world. It is eaten in Italy, Spain, Greece, and the South of France. People in these countries live longer and have fewer health problems than people in other countries. So what should you eat if you want to follow this diet?

◀ **Fruits and Vegetables**
Fruits and vegetables are good for your heart.
How often: every day

◀ **Fish**
Fish contains a lot of protein and is also good for your heart.
How often: at least twice a week

◀ **Beans**
Beans contain protein, vitamins, minerals, and fiber. There are many different varieties.
How often: at least three times a week

◀ **Herbs**
Herbs like oregano, rosemary, thyme, and bay contain healthy antioxidants.
How often: every day

◀ **Nuts and Seeds**
Nuts contain fats that are good for your heart.
How often: every day

◀ **Olive Oil**
Olive oil contains antioxidants and fats that are good for your heart.
How often: always, with every meal

◀ **Wine**
Red wine may help prevent heart disease.
How often: one small glass every day

 Discuss the questions with your partner.

1. How does the Mediterranean diet compare to your own diet? What are the similarities/differences?
2. Do you think the diet in your country is healthy? Why / Why not?

i Write

Write a description of the diet in your country. Say what is healthy and what isn't healthy about it.

I live in China. A lot of the food we eat is healthy, but there are also some things that are not healthy. We eat a lot of vegetables, which contain vitamins. We also eat a lot of tofu and fish, which have many health benefits. However, some Chinese food is fried and it sometimes contains a lot of sauce. It can be quite salty. Therefore, Chinese food is very healthy, as long as you choose the right things!

Lesson 9: Have you ever tried Mexican food?

Warm-Up

A Check (✓) the things that you have done. Then talk with your partner about what happened.

Have you ever ...?

- Have you ever won some money?
- Have you ever won an award? 
- Have you ever been in hospital? 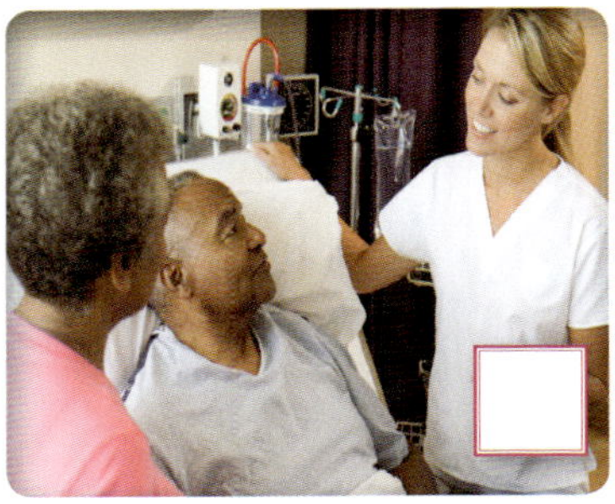
- Have you ever eaten any unusual foods? 
- Have you ever played a sport? 

B Check (✓) the things that you *have been doing*. Then complete the sentences to make them true for you. Talk with your partner about what you have been doing.

- ☐ I have been studying English for _____.
- ☐ I have been living in this city/town for _____.
- ☐ I have been dating my boyfriend/girlfriend for _____.
- ☐ I have been married for _____.

Dialogue 1 *Listen to the dialogue and practice.*

Gloria: Ian, let's eat out tonight. What do you feel like having?
Ian: Let's try something new. Have you ever tried Mexican food?
Gloria: Yes, I've eaten Mexican food many times.
Ian: Oh, really? What dishes have you tried?
Gloria: I've eaten burritos, tacos, and nachos. I love them all. Delicious!
Ian: Well I've never eaten Mexican food, but let's try something that is new for both of us. How about Turkish food? Have you eaten that recently?
Gloria: I haven't eaten Turkish food since I was in college. Actually, one of my former co-workers has just opened a new Turkish restaurant. She invited me to go there soon. She promised me the kebabs are great!
Ian: OK, let's go there then. I've never eaten a kebab, but I'd like to try one.
Gloria: Good idea. Let's meet there after work.
Ian: I'm looking forward to it already!

Comprehension Check!

1. What does Gloria suggest doing in the evening?
2. Has Ian eaten Mexican food before?
3. Has Gloria ever eaten Turkish food?

Language Focus 1

Life Experiences	
Have you (ever) tried Mexican food?	**Yes, I've tried** Mexican food. **No, I've never tried** Mexican food. Yes, **I have**. No, **I haven't**.
Have you eaten Turkish food **recently**?	**I haven't eaten** Turkish food **since** I was in college. Yes, **I ate** Turkish food last week.
What dishes have you eaten?	**I've eaten** burritos, tacos, and nachos.

Pronunciation

Past Tense Endings

Discover Pronunciation!
Listen to the extracts from Dialogue 1. Notice how the speakers pronounce the past tense ending -ed in three different ways.

Ian: Let's try something new. Have you ever tri**ed** [/d/] Mexican food?
Gloria: She invit**ed** [/ɪd/] me to go there soon. She promis**ed** [/t/] me the kebabs are great!

Pronounce -ed as /ɪd/ when the base form of the verb ends in /d/ or /t/.
Pronounce -ed as /t/ when the base form of the verb ends in /f/, /k/, /p/, /s/, /ʃ/, or /tʃ/.
Pronounce -ed as /d/ when the base form of the verb ends in other sounds.

Practice Pronunciation!
Say ONE sentence from each pair to your partner. Does your partner know which sentence you said?

❶ ⓐ They enjoy eating Mexican food.
  ⓑ They enjoyed eating Mexican food.

❷ ⓐ We always laugh a lot.
  ⓑ We always laughed a lot.

❸ ⓐ We start working at 9 o'clock.
  ⓑ We started working at 9 o'clock.

Talk 1

A Check (✓) the things that you have done recently.

What have you done recently?

☐ played soccer	☐ eaten Italian food	☐ been to Europe
☐ played pool	☐ eaten Chinese food	☐ been to the USA
☐ gone snowboarding/skiing	☐ eaten Vietnamese food	☐ been to Canada
☐ gone rafting	☐ eaten Indian food	☐ been to Japan
☐ ridden a horse	☐ eaten American food	☐ been to a tropical island

B Talk with your partner about what you *have* and *haven't done* recently, using the information in **A**.

Example
A: Have you played soccer recently?
B: Yes, I played last week. / No, I haven't played since last year.

Talk 2

 A Write five questions to ask your partner about his/her life experiences. Then ask your partner your questions. Write the answers.

> **Example**
> **A:** Have you ever been overseas?
> **B:** Yes, I have. I've been to Japan.

① Q: _____?
   A: _____.

② Q: _____?
   A: _____.

③ Q: _____?
   A: _____.

④ Q: _____?
   A: _____.

⑤ Q: _____?
   A: _____.

 B Tell the class what you found out about your partner.

> **Example**
> I found out that Mee-yeon has lived overseas, in New York. She has also been to Japan and Hong Kong. She hasn't been to a tropical island, but she'd like to. She likes winter sports; she has gone snowboarding and skiing. She has also worked out at a gym. She loves lots of different kinds of food. She has eaten Italian, Chinese, Vietnamese, and Thai food. Unfortunately, she has never won any money, but she has won an award.

Dialogue 2
Listen to the dialogue and practice.

Justin: Excuse me. Do you know what time the Number 24 is due? I've been waiting for over 45 minutes!
Rachel: The Number 24 is very unreliable. It's better to take the Number 30 from the bus station.
Justin: Oh, I didn't know that. Where is the bus station?
Rachel: It's just ten minutes from here. Are you new to the city?
Justin: Yes, I've recently moved here, so I've been commuting to work every day on the Number 24!
Rachel: Oh, no wonder you look tired and stressed! Take the Number 30 in future.
Justin: I will. Thanks for the advice. How long have you been living here?
Rachel: I've been living here for about ten years. The neighborhood has changed a lot in that time.
Justin: I'm sure it has. Actually, I've been hoping to meet some local people here. Would you like to have a coffee together sometime?
Rachel: Sure, why not? That would be nice.

Comprehension Check!
1. How does Justin look? Why?
2. How long has Rachel been living in the neighborhood?

Language Focus 2

Effects of Past Actions

Why do you look so stressed**?**	**I've been** wait**ing** for the bus for almost an hour.
Why are you so tired**?**	**I've been** commut**ing** to work every day.
Why are your clothes wet**?**	**I've been** walk**ing** in the rain.
How do you know about it?	**I've been** talk**ing** to Amanda.

Things That Began in the Past and Continue Until Now

How long have you been liv**ing** here**?**	**I've been** liv**ing** here **for** about ten years.
How long have you been study**ing** English**?**	**I've been** study**ing** English **for** five years.
Would you like to have a coffee together sometime**?**	Sure. **I've been** hop**ing** to meet someone like you.

Talk 3

Decide with your partner what the people in the pictures have been doing.

i Read

A Read the magazine article. What have the people done in their lives?

The Best Thing I've Ever Done

Joe, the traveler:

The best thing I've ever done is take a round-the-world trip. I've been to lots of countries in Europe, including Italy, Switzerland, and the UK. I've also been to the US, Canada, Mexico, and all over Asia. During my travels, I met many nice people who have since become my friends. By talking with them, I've been able to learn more about the different cultures of the world. I think this has made me a more open-minded person.

Monica, the adventurer:

I've been climbing mountains since I was 14. I've climbed Mount Everest, Mount Kilimanjaro, and lots of mountains in my home state of Colorado. I've met many great climbers since I started climbing. They have taught me a lot about climbing, and about life. I've also learned to cope with difficulties through climbing. Mountain climbing can be dangerous. I've broken a leg, and suffered frostbite several times. However, I keep climbing because I love the challenge and the natural beauty of the mountains.

B Discuss the questions with your partner.

1. Have you ever been overseas? Which countries have you been to?
2. If you could go on a round-the-world trip, which countries would you go to? What would you do there?
3. Have you ever gone mountain climbing? If you have, where did you go climbing? If you haven't, would you like to?
4. What is the best thing you've done in your life so far?

i Write

Write about something that you started recently and still do now. Choose one of the topics below, or use an idea of your own.

| take a course | be on a diet | work out | learn to cook/dance | work as a volunteer |

Example

I've been working out since January. After eating and drinking a lot at Christmas, I decided it was time to get into shape. I've been going to the gym three or four times a week. I've also been eating more healthily. I've lost a lot of weight already, and I feel happier and less stressed. Also, thanks to my new look, I've been getting more dates! I definitely recommend working out.

Lesson 10
Where shall we go on vacation this year?

Warm-Up

 Match the words with the pictures.

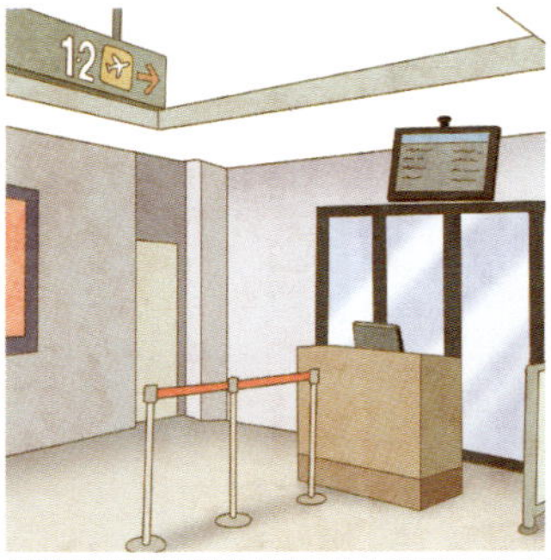

immigration	check-in counter	gate	baggage claim
window seat	aisle seat	overhead bin	flight attendant

 Discuss the questions with your partner.
1. Have you ever taken a flight? Describe the process of taking a flight, using the words above.
2. Do you enjoy flying? Why / Why not?
3. Which countries/cities have you flown to? Why did you go there?

Dialogue 1
Listen to the dialogue and practice.

Staff: Southwestern Airlines. How can I help you today?
Caller: Hello. I'd like to book a return ticket to Amsterdam, please. And I'd like a direct flight. I don't want to transfer.
Staff: OK, sir. When would you like to leave?
Caller: I'd like to leave on July 14.
Staff: And what date would you like to return?
Caller: Two weeks later, on July 28.
Staff: Would you like to fly business or economy class?
Caller: I'll take economy class, please.
Staff: OK. Please bear with me while I check our computer system. [pause] Yes, there are seats available on the dates you request. The outbound flight departs at 8:30 pm, and the return flight is at 4:15 pm. Is that OK for you?
Caller: Yes, those times are fine. I'd like to go ahead and reserve those flights, please.
Staff: No problem. I can do that for you. First, could you tell me your name and telephone number, please?
Caller: Sure. It's Peter Jackson. 555-2326-118.

Comprehension Check!

1. Where does the caller want to go?
2. On what dates and at what times will he travel?

Language Focus 1

Reserving a Flight

Southwestern Airlines. **How can/may I help you?**	I'd like to book a return/round-trip/one-way ticket from Mumbai to Amsterdam, please.
When would you like to leave/return/fly? **What date would you like to leave/return/fly?** **What dates would you like?**	I'd like to leave/return/fly on July 14.
Would you like a direct or an indirect flight?	I'd like a direct flight. It doesn't matter. I'd like a stopover in Singapore.
Would you like to fly business, economy, or first class?	I'll take economy class/business class/ first class, please.
The outbound flight departs at 8:30 pm, **and the return flight is at** 4:15 pm. **Is that OK for you?**	Yes, those times are fine. I'd like to go ahead and reserve those flights, please. Unfortunately those times don't work for me. Are there any later/earlier flights?

Talk 1

A Complete the notes with information about the flights you want to book.

→ _____
late evening
July 8
direct

London ↔ _____
early morning
_____

New York ← _____
_____ → Dubai
September 18
stopover

→ _____
late evening
November 24

_____ ← _____
→ _____

B Imagine that your partner is an airline booking agent. Roleplay conversations, using the information in **A**.

> **Example**
> **A:** Southwestern Airlines. How can I help you?
> **B:** I'd like to book a return ticket from New York to Dubai, please.
> **A:** OK, madam. Would you like a direct or an indirect flight?

Talk 2

A Ask three classmates who have taken flights questions to complete the table below.

> **Example**
> **A:** Where did you fly to?
> **B:** I flew to Singapore.
> **A:** Was it a direct or an indirect flight?

	1	2	3
Name			
Destination			
Time of Day			
Direct/Indirect/Stopover			
Any Further Information			

B Tell the class what you found out about your classmates.

Dialogue 2 *Listen to the dialogue and practice.*

Angela: Sam, where shall we go on vacation this year? Have you been thinking about it?
Sam: No, I haven't. Hmm … there are so many places I'd like to go. It's difficult to decide.
Angela: Exactly. How about visiting a city? We could go to Rome, Paris, Athens …? That would be nice.
Sam: I don't agree. I'd prefer to go somewhere like Bali.
Angela: Why? Do you think a city vacation would be too expensive?
Sam: Yes, it would be expensive, but that's not the point. I want to have a relaxing vacation. I think we need to relax.
Angela: You're right. I think so, too. But surely Bali is too far away.
Sam: I don't think so. The flight to Bali takes just five hours.
Angela: Oh, I see. So what can we do in Bali?
Sam: Well, on the first day we can relax on the beach. The next day, we can do some water sports, like scuba diving or surfing.
Angela: That sounds really fun! Why don't we get a massage, too?
Sam: Absolutely! We can get a massage on the third day. Then, on the fourth day we can go paragliding. And on the last day, maybe we can do some shopping or take a tour.
Angela: That sounds perfect. Let's do it!

Comprehension Check!

❶ What does Angela suggest?
❷ Where does Sam want to go? What does he want to do there?

Language Focus 2

Making Suggestions / Planning
How about go**ing** to Bali**?**
Why don't we get a massage**?**
On the first/second/third/fourth/final day, we can relax on the beach**.**

Agreeing	Disagreeing
Yes, that's/you're right.	I don't think so.
I think so, too.	I don't agree.
Exactly.	I'd prefer not to.
I (totally) agree with you.	That's not the point/problem.
Absolutely!	But **surely** that's too far away.

 **Pronunciation**

Questions 1

Discover Pronunciation!
Listen to the extracts from Dialogue 1 and Dialogue 2. Notice how the speakers' voices rise or fall when they ask questions.

Staff: Southwestern Airlines. How can I help you today? ↘
Caller: Hello. I'd like to book a return ticket to Amsterdam, please.

Caller: Would you like to fly business or economy class? ↗
Staff: I'll take economy class, please.

Angela: Sam, where shall we go on vacation this year? Have you been thinking about it? ↗
Sam: No, I haven't.

Angela: Why? Do you think a city vacation would be too expensive? ↗
Sam: Yes, it would be expensive, but that's not the point.

When the answer to a question can be *yes* or *no*, the speaker's voice rises (↗). When the question is open, and *yes* or *no* cannot be the answer, the speaker's voice falls (↘).

Practice Pronunciation!
Read the dialogue. Decide whether the speakers' voices should rise or fall after each question. Write ↗ or ↘ in each gap. Then practice the dialogue with your partner.

A: What shall we do during our vacation? ▭
B: Hmm. Do you like scuba diving? ▭
A: No, not really. I prefer to do something more relaxing. What relaxing things can we do? ▭
B: Well, why don't we go sunbathing? Do you agree? ▭
A: Yes, let's do that.

Talk 3

A Work in groups. Agree on FIVE things to do during a five-day vacation.

Example
A: How about going sunbathing?
B: I'd prefer not to. Sunbathing is boring. Why don't we do something more active, like go scuba diving?

- go sunbathing ☐
- sail on a yacht ☐
- go scuba diving ☐
- go paragliding ☐
- take a tour ☐

- take a cruise ☐
- go rafting ☐
- relax on the beach ☐
- go shopping ☐
- read some books ☐

B Work in new groups. Suggest doing the activities you chose in **A**. Agree on what to do each day during your vacation.

HOLIDAY PLANNER

DAY 1

DAY 2

DAY 3

DAY 4

DAY 5

i Read

A Read the magazine article. Which destination would you most like to visit? Why?

This Year's Top Tourist Destinations

◀ **Brazil**
Brazil is a fantastic place to visit. It is the largest country in South America, and the fifth largest in the world, so there is a lot to do. In Rio de Janeiro, you can enjoy beautiful beaches and the annual carnival. Away from the city, nature lovers can explore the Amazon rainforest. In the rainforest you can see lots of rare animals, such as the jaguar and the boa constrictor snake, and beautiful natural scenery like the Iguassu Falls.

◀ **Singapore**
Singapore is a small place, but it has a lot to offer. In the city, you can eat tasty food and go shopping. You can also visit beautiful gardens and parks. Nearby, on Sentosa Island, you can relax on clean beaches and enjoy a variety of water sports. There is also an oceanarium where you can see dolphins and tropical fish.

◀ **Switzerland**
Switzerland is one of the most famous tourist destinations in the world. The Swiss Alps are a paradise for people who love winter sports, with some of the best skiing and snowboarding in the world. You can also enjoy some fantastic views of mountains and lakes. If you visit Switzerland, you should stay in a chalet (a traditional wooden house), where you will feel warm and comfortable.

B Discuss the questions with your partner.

1. Do you have any vacation plans? Where will you go and what will you do there?
2. What is the best/worst tourist destination that you have visited? Describe it.
3. In your opinion, what makes a place a good tourist destination?
4. Which places in your country would you recommend to visitors?

i Write

A Read the e-mail from Paula. Where is she? What is she doing there?

From: Paula
To: You
Subject: having a great time in London
Date: August 15, 22:18

Hi,
How are you doing?
I'm having a great time here in London. Yesterday was a beautiful sunny day so I went to the London Eye. The view of London from the top of the Eye is stunning. I could see the Houses of Parliament, the Millennium Dome, and all of London's other famous buildings. Yesterday, I also visited Buckingham Palace and bought a cute teddy bear. London was pretty busy yesterday due to the nice weather. Usually it rains here!
How about you? Are you enjoying your trip? What have you done there? And how's the weather? I'm looking forward to hearing all your news soon!
Miss you.

B Imagine that you are a tourist on vacation in your country. Write a reply to Paula to tell her about your trip.

Lesson 11

What did it taste like?

Warm-Up

A Match the countries and foods with the pictures. Then write some of the ingredients used in the foods.

① Country:
Food:
Ingredients:

② Country:
Food:
Ingredients:

③ Country:
Food:
Ingredients:

④ Country:
Food:
Ingredients:

⑤ Country:
Food:
Ingredients:

⑥ Country:
Food:
Ingredients:

Countries			Foods		
India	Italy	Mexico	burrito	curry	fondue
Spain	Switzerland	Vietnam	paella	pho	spaghetti bolognese

B Discuss the questions with your partner.

① Which of the foods above have you tried? Did you like them? Why / Why not?
② Are there any other foods that you like from other countries? Describe them.

Dialogue 1 — Listen to the dialogue and practice.

Matt: Guess what I ate last night. Alligator!
Anna: Wow! Did you like it?
Matt: Yes, it was pretty good.
Anna: What did it taste like?
Matt: It tasted a little bit like chicken.
Anna: Oh, I've never tried it. How was it cooked? And what was it served with?
Matt: It was grilled, and served with vegetables and a delicious spicy sauce. You should try it sometime. What's the most unusual food you've ever eaten?
Anna: Well, when I was in Australia I ate kangaroo.
Matt: Oh really? What was it like? I heard it also tastes like chicken.
Anna: No, you can't compare it with chicken. It wasn't as tender as chicken. It tasted more like steak to me.
Matt: I see. And how was it cooked? Was it roasted?
Anna: No. It was barbecued.
Matt: And what did it come with?
Anna: It came with rice.
Matt: Did you like it?
Anna: No, I wasn't keen on it. It was kind of tough and chewy. I wouldn't choose it again.

Comprehension Check!

1. What unusual foods did Matt and Anna eat?
2. Did they like the foods? Why / Why not?

Language Focus 1

Asking for Information and Making Comparisons

What did it taste like? What was it like?	It tasted a bit like chicken/fish/potato. It wasn't as tender/juicy/spicy as chicken/lamb/curry. You can't compare kangaroo with chicken. It tasted more like steak.
How was it cooked?	It was grilled/barbecued/roasted/baked/steamed/fried.
What was it served with? What did it come with? What did you eat it with?	It was served with / It came with / I ate it with vegetables / a sauce / a salad / fries.

Likes and Dislikes

Did you like it? How did you like it?	✓ Yes, it was delicious. ✓ It was pretty good. ✗ I wasn't keen on it. It was tough / chewy / salty / greasy / too spicy. ✗ I wouldn't choose it again.

Talk 1

A Discuss the questions with your partner.

 What is the most unusual food you've ever eaten?
 What unusual food would you like to eat?

B Tell the class what you found out about your partner.

 I found out that Michael has eaten rabbit. He says it tastes like chicken. It was served with rice and vegetables.
⋮

Pronunciation

Questions 2

Discover Pronunciation!

Listen to the extracts from Dialogue 1. Notice how the speakers' voices rise or fall when they ask questions.

Anna: Wow! Did you like it? ↗
Matt: Yes, it was pretty good.
Anna: What did it taste like? ↘
Matt: It tasted a little bit like chicken.

Matt: And what did it come with? ↘
Anna: It came with rice.
Matt: Did you like it? ↗
Anna: No, I wasn't keen on it. It was kind of tough and chewy. I wouldn't choose it again.

Remember that when the answer to a question can be *yes* or *no*, the speaker's voice rises (↗). When the question is open, and *yes* or *no* cannot be the answer, the speaker's voice falls (↘).

Practice Pronunciation!

A Write answers to the questions.

1. **A:** What did you have for dinner last night?
   B: _____.

2. **A:** Have you ever eaten kangaroo?
   B: _____.

3. **A:** What time do you usually eat dinner?
   B: _____.

4. **A:** Is there a restaurant near your home?
   B: _____.

5. **A:** Who cooked your dinner last night?
   B: _____.

B Decide whether Speaker A's voice should rise or fall after each question in **A**. Write ↗ or ↘ after each question. Then practice the dialogues with your partner.

Dialogue 2
Listen to the dialogue and practice.

Ryan: Hi, Alice. How was your trip to India?
Alice: Oh, it was fantastic. I stayed with an Indian family, so I learned a lot about Indian customs.
Ryan: Oh, really? Like what?
Alice: Well, the main thing I noticed was that Indian people usually don't use cutlery. They eat with their hands. Sometimes they use a spoon, but never a knife or fork. Also, you must always use your right hand, never the left.
Ryan: I never knew that. What else did you learn?
Alice: I discovered that table manners are very important to Indians. The eldest person starts eating first. Everyone else has to wait. Also, no one can leave the table until the eldest person has finished their food.
Ryan: I see. And what about meat? I heard a lot of Indians are vegetarians.
Alice: There are a lot of vegetarians, but many people eat meat. They don't eat beef though.
Ryan: I see. And do Indian people sit on the floor to eat, or at a table?
Alice: Sometimes they sit on the floor, sometimes at a table. When they sit on the floor, they always sit with their legs crossed. At a table, they sit with their backs straight. I realized that this is very important.

Comprehension Check!
1. Where did Alice go?
2. What did she learn about eating customs there?

Language Focus 2

Talking About What You Have Learned

I found out that Indian people often eat with their hands.
I learnt/learned that Indian food is spicy.
I discovered that the eldest person eats first.
I realized that table manners are important in India.
It became clear that Indian people eat a lot of vegetables.
The main thing I noticed was that people often sit on the floor to eat.

Talk 2

Discuss the questions with your partner.

1. What is your favorite traditional meal in your country? Think about:
   - What are the ingredients?
   - Where do you usually eat it?
   - How do you eat it?
   - What is it served with?

2. What are the eating customs in your country? Describe them, comparing your country with India.

	India	My Country
Cutlery		
Table Manners		
Ingredients		

Talk 3

A Work in three groups. Read the instructions for your group and prepare some questions.

Group A: Find out which foods your classmates dislike.
Group B: Find out which meals your classmates can cook.
Group C: Find out which drinks your classmates like and dislike.

Question(s):

Name	Answer

B Ask four classmates your questions. Then tell your group what you found out about your classmates.

Example: The main thing I noticed was that everybody can cook noodles.

i Read

A Read the blog entry. What is the most popular food in the UK?

> traveler_joe
> March 17
>
> Europe UK
> ### UK Food
>
> I'm learning a lot about British food here in the UK. Last night, I ate fish and chips for the first time. To be honest, I wouldn't choose it again. The fried fish was kind of greasy.
>
> Another popular dish that I tried is the traditional English breakfast: sausages, bacon, mushrooms, eggs, and fried tomatoes. The breakfast is usually served with toast and coffee or tea. It's pretty good, although, again, quite greasy. It's not as nice as the breakfasts I had in America, but it's not bad.
>
> My favorite English food is also the most surprising: chicken tikka masala. It's a curry that was created in England by Indian immigrants. It's now the most popular dish in the UK! It's delicious. Usually it's served with rice and Indian bread. I also tried some lamb curries, but lamb isn't as tender as chicken, so I'm not keen on it.

fish and chips

English breakfast

chicken tikka masala

B Discuss the questions with your partner.

1. Which foods has the writer tried in the UK?
2. Which foods did the writer like and dislike? Why?

i Write

Imagine that you are a foreign visitor to your country. Write a blog entry about the food in the country.

Lesson 12

Hello. Is Tim there?

Warm-Up

A Match the pictures with the descriptions.

Phones and Technology

❶ smartphone

❷ video calling

❸ keyphone

❹ video conferencing

❺ rotary telephone

❻ walkie-talkie

ⓐ It was developed in the late 19th century and was the standard telephone design until the launch of the push-button telephone.

ⓑ It has extra buttons that allow incoming calls to be transferred to other extensions. It is commonly used in companies.

ⓒ It enables you to chat face to face with family and friends. It is free and all you need is a computer, webcam, and internet connection.

ⓓ It was created in 1940 and was used for military communication during World War Two.

ⓔ It combines the functions of a camera phone and a handheld computer. Users can install and run applications.

ⓕ It allows people in different locations to hold face-to-face meetings. It uses computer networks to send audio and video data.

B Discuss the questions with your partner.

❶ Which of the methods of communication in **A** have you used? Did you enjoy using them? Why / Why not?

❷ What features would you like telephones to have in the future?

Dialogue 1
Listen to the dialogue and practice.

Receptionist: Good morning. Stardom Technologies. How may I help you?
Mr Tyler: Yes, this is Gene Tyler from Global Communications. May I speak to Mr Sam Brown, please?
Receptionist: I'm sorry, but he's not in the office right now.
Mr Tyler: What time do you expect him back?
Receptionist: He'll be back by 3. May I take a message?
Mr Tyler: Yes, please. Could you ask him to call me on my cell phone?
Receptionist: Sure. May I have your cell phone number?
Mr Tyler: It's 313-555-4917.
Receptionist: Let me repeat that just to make sure. 313-555-4917.
Mr Tyler: That's correct.
Receptionist: OK, Mr Tyler. I'll make sure Mr Brown gets the message. Thank you for calling.
Mr Tyler: All right. Thank you. Goodbye.
Receptionist: Goodbye.

Comprehension Check!
1. Who does Mr Tyler call? Why?
2. What will the receptionist do for Mr Tyler?

Language Focus 1

Formal Telephone Language

May I speak to Mr Brown?	He is not in the office right now.
May I take a message?	Yes. Could you ask him to call me, please?
Would you like to leave a message?	Yes. Please tell him (that) his brother called.
May I ask who's calling?	This is / It's Terry Braun.
Would you mind spelling your last name?	It's B-R-A-U-N.

Talk 1

Practice with your partner, completing the sentences to make them true for you.

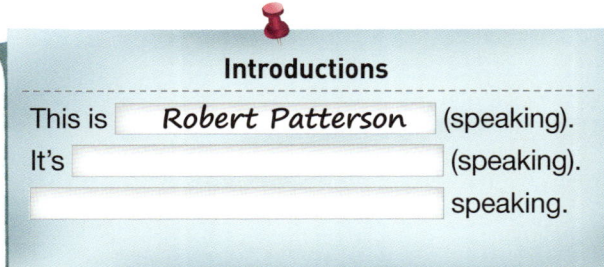

Introductions
This is Robert Patterson (speaking).
It's _____ (speaking).
_____ speaking.

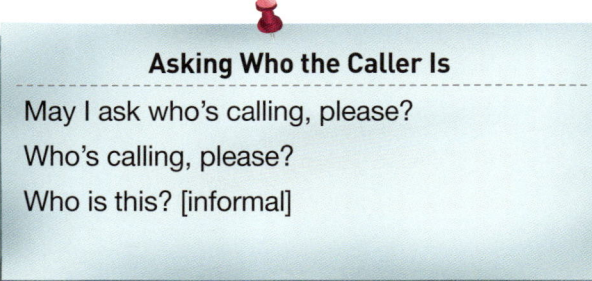

Asking Who the Caller Is
May I ask who's calling, please?
Who's calling, please?
Who is this? [informal]

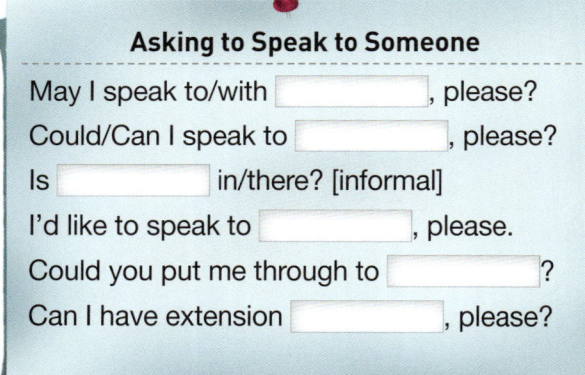

Asking to Speak to Someone
May I speak to/with ____, please?
Could/Can I speak to ____, please?
Is ____ in/there? [informal]
I'd like to speak to ____, please.
Could you put me through to ____?
Can I have extension ____, please?

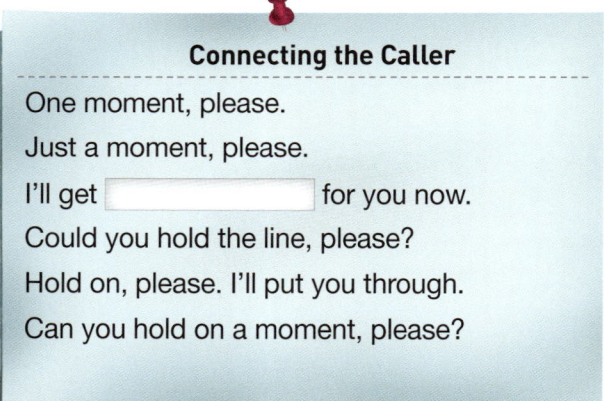

Connecting the Caller
One moment, please.
Just a moment, please.
I'll get ____ for you now.
Could you hold the line, please?
Hold on, please. I'll put you through.
Can you hold on a moment, please?

 **Pronunciation**

Reductions of H- Words

Discover Pronunciation!

The /h/ sound is often removed in *him* and *her*. Speakers link *him* and *her* closely with the previous sounds.

Written	Spoken
Did you see **him**?	Did you see **him**?
I like **her** a lot.	I like **her** a lot.
What did **he** do?	What did **he** do?
What's **her** name?	What's **her** name?

Practice Pronunciation!

Listen to the sentences from Dialogue 1. Notice how the speakers pronounce the highlighted words. Then practice the sentences with your partner.

① I'm sorry, **but he's** not in the office right now.
② What time do you **expect him** back?
③ Could you **ask him** to call me on my cell phone?
④ OK, Mr Tyler. I'll make **sure he** gets the message.

Dialogue 2 — Listen to the dialogue and practice.

Tim: Hello?
Ron: Hello. Is Tim there?
Tim: Speaking. Who is this?
Ron: It's Ron calling.
Tim: Hi, Ron. It's good to hear your voice. What's up?
Ron: I'm calling about the study group you're leading. I was wondering if I could join your group.
Tim: Sure, you're more than welcome to join us. We're meeting at Leslie's tomorrow. You know where she lives, right?
Ron: Sort of. Could you give me her address?
Tim: Hold on a second. [pause] Here you go. It's 7211 37th Street. Please be there by 7 pm.
Ron: OK, I've got it all down. That's only two blocks from my place. I'll be there.
Tim: Well, I'll see you tomorrow, then. Looking forward to it. Bye for now!
Ron: Thank you so much, Tim. Take care and see you soon.

Comprehension Check!

1. Why does Ron call Tim?
2. Who is Leslie? Where does she live?

Language Focus 2

	Informal Telephone Language
Is Tim **there?**	Yes. **Hang on one second, please.**
Is Maria **in?**	**Just a moment. I'll get her.**
Who is this?	**It's** Sean **calling.**
Hold on.	OK. Thanks.
Say that again?	**Please tell her to** meet me at the library.

Talk 2

Roleplay a conversation with your partner, using the sentences.

When Someone is Not Available

I'm sorry. _____ is not available at the moment.

_____ is not in.

He/She is out to lunch right now.

He/She just stepped out.

The line is busy.

Taking a Message

May/Could/Can I take a message?

Would you like to leave a message?

Would you like to call later?

Asking for Information

May I have your name and phone number, please?

Could you spell that for me, please?

What was your address again?

Could you repeat that, please?

Confirming Information

Let me repeat that just to make sure.

So it's S-I-M-P-S-O-N?

Did you say 8412 Western Avenue?

OK, I've got it all down.

Talk 3

Match the telephone-related problems with the expressions.

Problems

- ☐ It's a bad connection, so it's hard to hear.
- ☐ The caller didn't understand what the other person said.
- ☐ The caller is speaking too quickly.
- ☐ The caller is speaking too quietly.
- ☐ The caller has the wrong number.
- ☐ There's a lot of background noise, so it's hard to hear.

Expressions

1. I'm sorry, but you have the wrong number.
2. Could you speak a little more slowly, please?
3. Could you speak up a little, please?
4. Could you call me back? I think we have a bad connection.
5. Could you repeat that, please?
6. I can hardly hear you. There's a lot of background noise.

i Read

A Read the voicemail messages. Which person can be contacted by cell phone?

Voicemail 1
Hi. This is Sophia. I'm sorry, but I'm not available to take your call at this time. Please leave your name, number, and a brief message. I'll get back to you as soon as I can. Thank you.

Voicemail 2
Hello. You have reached Thomas Young's voicemail. I am currently out of the office on business. Please leave your name and telephone number, and I will return your call as soon as I can when I get back. If you need to speak with me immediately, please press 3 to reach my cell phone. Thank you.

Voicemail 3
Hello, this is Jonathan Hernandez. Today is April 6. I will be in meetings all day. Your call is important to me. If you leave a detailed message, I will return your call at my first opportunity. If your call is urgent, press 0 for assistance. Thank you.

Voicemail 4
Thank you for calling Dr Lee's office. Our hours are 9 am to 5 pm, Monday through Friday. Please call back during these hours, or leave a message after the beep. If this is an emergency, please call 701-555-2080, or go to a hospital emergency room.

B Discuss the questions with your partner.

1. What does Sophia ask the caller to do?
2. Why is Thomas Young out of the office?
3. What is Jonathan Hernandez doing all day?
4. When is Dr Lee's office available to take calls?

i Write

A Write a message in response to one of the voicemail messages in i Read.

B Imagine that you will be away for a week. Write a voicemail message.

Lesson 13
I'd like to make an appointment for a haircut.

Warm-Up

A Complete the sentences, using the appropriate words from the list. Refer to the pictures.

My car broke down. I need a/an _____.

I want a facial. I need a/an _____.

My sink is blocked. I need a/an _____.

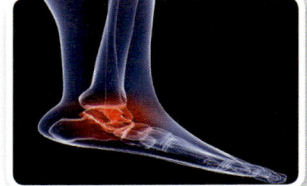
I sprained my ankle. I need a/an _____.

My partner breached our contract. I need a/an _____.

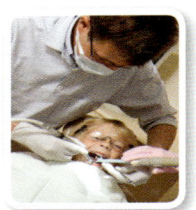
My gum is swollen. I need a/an _____.

| dentist | plumber | orthopedic surgeon |
| lawyer | mechanic | esthetician |

B Imagine that you are an internationally famous conference speaker. Complete your schedule.

Conference Schedule

Date	Time	Location
March 12	10:30 am	Albany, NY, USA
		Houston, TX, USA
		Toronto, Canada
		Seoul, Korea
		Warsaw, Poland
		Guadalajara, Mexico

Dialogue 1 Listen to the dialogue and practice.

Receptionist: Good morning. Super Hair Salon. How may I help you?
Jenny: Hello. I'd like to make an appointment for a haircut.
Receptionist: OK. What day would you like to come in?
Jenny: I'd like to come in on Friday.
Receptionist: OK. We have openings in the morning only. Could you come in at 11 am?
Jenny: Can I come in a little later?
Receptionist: I could fit you in at 11:30.
Jenny: OK. That's fine for me.
Receptionist: Could I take your name and phone number, please?
Jenny: My name is Jenny Lu. That's L-U, and my phone number is 555-4573.
Receptionist: OK, Jenny. We'll see you on Friday. If you can't come in for any reason, please give me a call.
Jenny: Sounds great. Thank you very much. Bye!
Receptionist: Goodbye.

Comprehension Check!

1. Why did Jenny call the hair salon?
2. If Jenny can't go to the salon, what should she do?

Language Focus 1

Making Appointments 1

I'd like to make an appointment for a haircut.
I'd like to make an appointment with a doctor.
I'd like to come (in) on Friday.
Can I come (in) on Friday?
Could you come (in) at 11 am?
Can we make it 2:30 pm?
I can/can't make it tomorrow.

Talk 1

Ask four classmates questions about their appointments this week to complete the table.

Example

A: Maria, what appointments do you have this week?
B: I'm having lunch with some friends on April 25.
A: Which restaurant are you going to?
B: We're going to Pizza Italiana.
A: What time are you meeting?
B: At 1 pm.

Name	Date	Time	Place	With	Purpose
Maria Garcia	April 25	1 pm	Pizza Italiana	friends	lunch

Dialogue 2
Listen to the dialogue and practice.

Samantha: Professor, can I make an appointment with you? Finals are coming up, and I need some help.
Professor: All right. I will be available on Wednesday afternoon from 2:30 until 4:30.
Samantha: 3 would be the best time.
Professor: Sounds great. You know where my office is, right?
Samantha: I think I do. It's in the Harold Reese Building, isn't it?
Professor: That's right. It's on the second floor, down the hall on the left.
Samantha: I'm sure I'll find it. I'll see you on Wednesday. Thank you very much.
Professor: My pleasure. If you can't make it, please give me a call.
Samantha: No problem. I'll be there.
Professor: Fine. See you then.
Samantha: Looking forward to it. Goodbye!

Comprehension Check!

1. Why does Samantha want to see the professor?
2. Where is the professor's office located?

Language Focus 2

Making Appointments 2

I'll be free on Wednesday afternoon.
I'll be available tomorrow morning.
Is next Tuesday **OK?**
What about this Saturday?
Can we meet sometime later today?
That will be fine.

Pronunciation

Contractions With *Will*

Discover Pronunciation!
Listen to the sentences and practice saying them.

I will	➡	I'll	I'll see you on Wednesday.
You will	➡	You'll	You'll be fine.
He will	➡	He'll	He'll be late today.
She will	➡	She'll	She'll understand.
It will	➡	It'll	It'll be raining tomorrow.
We will	➡	We'll	We'll get together sometime.
They will	➡	They'll	They'll be home by then.
Who will	➡	Who'll	Who'll you be seeing tonight?
That will	➡	That'll	That'll be fine.
What will	➡	What'll	What'll happen next?
Nick will	➡	Nick'll	Nick'll give me a nickel.

Practice Pronunciation!
Complete the sentences, then practice them with your partner.

❶ ⬜ 'll I do?
❷ ⬜ 'll we meet?
❸ ⬜ 'll be all.
❹ ⬜ 'll let you know.
❺ ⬜ 'll take some time.

Talk 2

Follow the four steps with your partner to arrange appointments 1–3.

❶ go see a movie on the weekend
❷ go hiking
❸ have dinner together

Step 1	Propose a time and place.
Step 2	Negotiate a meeting time and place.
Step 3	Suggest a different time/place.
Step 4	Agree the appointment.

Talk 3

A 🎧 Listen to the dialogue and check (✓) the correct options. Then add the appointment to the schedule.

❶ William called	☐ Dr Sanderson's office.	☐ Dr Simpson's office.
❷ William is busy on	☐ Monday.	☐ Tuesday.
❸ The doctor can see him on	☐ Wednesday.	☐ Friday.

	Mon	Tue	Wed	Thu	Fri
10 am	Jack Morris 555-2350		Rachel Gomez 302-9328	Julie Adams 556-3142	weekly seminar
11 am					
12 pm	lunch		lunch	lunch	lunch
1 pm	Ron Stewart 556-8459	doctors' conference		Andy Nelson 302-1849	
2 pm			Jason Kim 555-0428		
3 pm	Susan Hill 302-4769				
4 pm					

B 🎧 Listen again and complete the dialogue. Then practice the dialogue with your partner.

Receptionist: Good morning. Dr Simpson's office. How may I help you?
William: Hello, I'd like to _____ to see the doctor. Can he see me next Tuesday?
Receptionist: I am afraid not. He'll be out of the clinic all day. _____ on Monday afternoon?
William: No, I can't. _____ is a busy day for me. Is he free on Wednesday afternoon?
Receptionist: Let's see. _____ 3 pm? Will that be OK with you?
William: Yes. Wednesday at 3 pm is good for me.
Receptionist: Sounds good. Your _____ name and phone number, please.
William: My first name is William, and my surname is Carter: C-A-R-T-E-R. My phone number is 332-7086.

i Read

Read the e-mails, then discuss the questions with your partner.

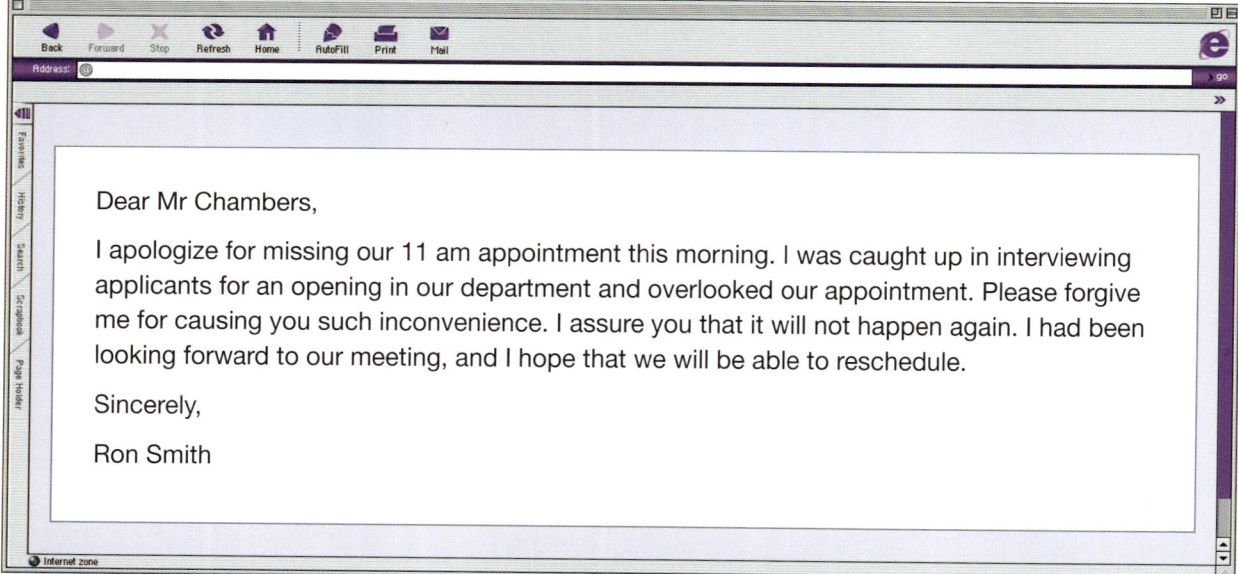

Dear Mr Chambers,

I apologize for missing our 11 am appointment this morning. I was caught up in interviewing applicants for an opening in our department and overlooked our appointment. Please forgive me for causing you such inconvenience. I assure you that it will not happen again. I had been looking forward to our meeting, and I hope that we will be able to reschedule.

Sincerely,

Ron Smith

❶ Why did Ron e-mail Mr Chambers?
❷ What is Ron's excuse?
❸ Do you think the meeting will be rescheduled? Why / Why not?

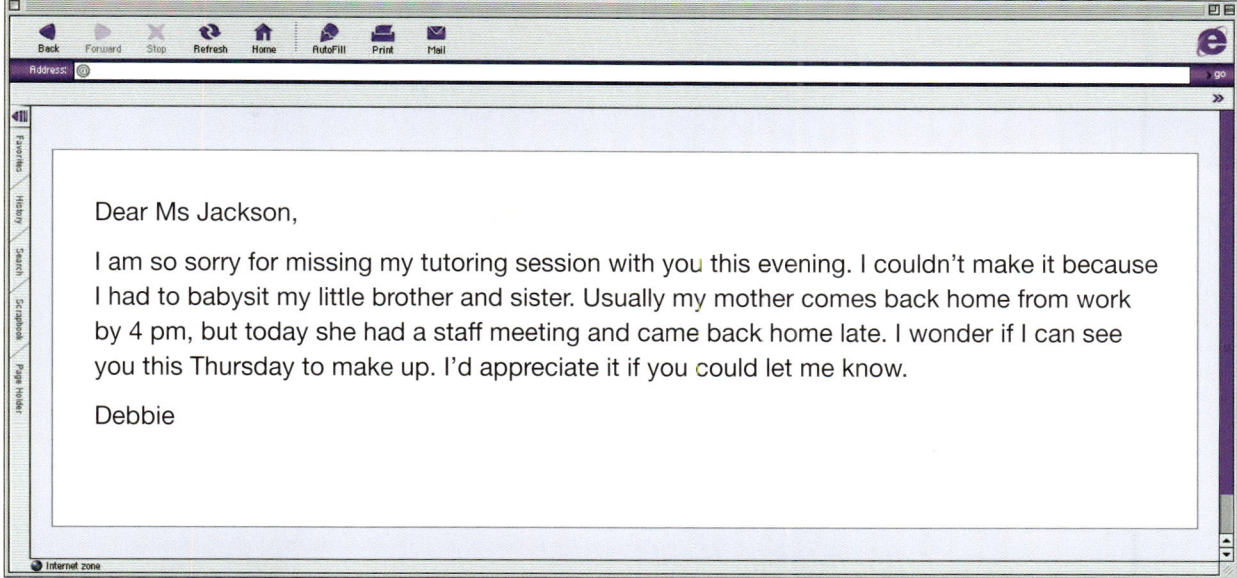

❹ What do you think is the relationship between Debbie and Ms Jackson?
❺ Why couldn't Debbie meet Ms Jackson?
❻ Have you ever missed an appointment? Tell your partner what happened.

i Write

Write e-mails in response to the e-mails in i Read.

Lesson 14　I think we have some problems.

Warm-Up

A Complete the sentences, using the appropriate words from the box.

| give me some money | being late | turning down the volume | apologize |

B Discuss the questions with your partner.

1. Have you ever been in any of the situations shown in **A**? What did you say and do? Or, what would you say and do?
2. What other things have you asked or apologized for recently? What did you say?

Dialogue 1
Listen to the dialogue and practice.

Stephanie: We've been sharing this apartment for three months now. Unfortunately, I think we have some problems.
Jessica: Yes, I agree. I think we should discuss the problems.
Stephanie: Right. As we're all here now, this is a good time to talk.
Paul: OK. May I go first?
Stephanie: Go ahead.
Paul: I often find your dirty dishes in the kitchen. Sometimes the sink is full of dishes. Could you possibly wash your dishes after you finish eating?
Jessica: Sure. No problem.
Stephanie: Yes, of course. Another problem, Paul, is that you have so many parties here. The occasional party is fine with us, but sometimes we need to sleep. So, we were wondering if you could have fewer parties.
Paul: Sure. And Jessica, would you mind keeping your cat in your room? There is cat hair all over the house.
Jessica: No, I'm afraid I can't. Mr Stripes needs a lot of space to walk around. Could you keep your bedroom door closed? That way he won't be able to get into your room.
Paul: OK, I'll do that.

Comprehension Check!
1. What three problems do the speakers mention?
2. Who is Mr Stripes? Does Paul like him? Why / Why not?

Language Focus 1

Requests and Replies	
May I go first**?**	Sure, go ahead.
	Sure.
Could you (possibly) wash your dishes after you finish eating**?**	Sure. No problem.
We were wondering if you could have fewer parties.	Yes, of course.
We wonder if you could wash your dishes.	OK, I'll do that.
Would you mind keep**ing** your cat in your room**?**	No, I'm afraid I can't.
	I'm sorry, but I can't.

 ## Pronunciation

Short Words

Discover Pronunciation!
Listen to the extracts from Dialogue 1 and Dialogue 2. Notice how the speakers pronounce the highlighted words.

Stephanie: We've been sharing this apartment **for** three months now. Unfortunately, I think we have **some** problems.
Jessica: Yes, I agree. I think we should discuss **the** problems.
Paul: Sometimes **the** sink is full **of** dishes.
Stephanie: The occasional party is fine with us, but sometimes we need **to** sleep.
Jessica: Mr Stripes needs **a** lot **of** space **to** walk around.

Short words (*a*, *and*, *as*, *for*, *of*, *or*, *some*, *the*, and *to*) are usually unstressed.

Practice Pronunciation!
Practice the sentences with your partner. Do not stress the highlighted words.

① **The** sink is full **of** dishes.
② I need **a** lot **of** space **for** my work.
③ Could you turn down **the** music, please? I'm trying **to** study.
④ I'm sorry **for** being late.
⑤ I need **some** money **to** take **a** bus.

Talk 1

A Order the irritating roommates 1–8, 1 being the most annoying, and 8 the least annoying.

The Most Irritating Roommates

The roommate who always has parties. ☐

The roommate who never washes the dishes. ☐

The roommate who speaks a different language. ☐

The roommate who has an annoying pet. ☐

The roommate who never goes out. ☐

The roommate who is unhygienic. ☐

The roommate who likes to walk around without many clothes on. ☐

The roommate who plays loud music in his/her room. ☐

B Roleplay conversations with your partner between two roommates. Use the information in **A**.

> Example
>
> **A:** We've been sharing this apartment for a month now. Unfortunately, I think we have some problems.
> **B:** Yes, I agree. I think we should discuss the problems.
> **A:** You always have parties. Would you mind having fewer parties?

Dialogue 2 *Listen to the dialogue and practice.*

Josie:	Hello, Mr Miller. It's Josie. Sorry to disturb you.
Mr Miller:	Don't worry, Josie. How can I help you?
Josie:	I'm calling about the apartment. Can you help us with some problems?
Mr Miller:	I'll do my best. What are the problems?
Josie:	Well firstly, the boiler seems to be out of order. I just took a freezing cold shower!
Mr Miller:	Oh dear. I'm terribly sorry about that. I'll look into the problem today. Shall I send a repair man today?
Josie:	Yes, please. Also, Mr Miller, we're having problems with the air conditioning. It won't turn on.
Mr Miller:	Actually, the air conditioning unit is quite old. I'm planning to replace it soon. I'm afraid I don't have enough money this month. I do apologize. Do you mind waiting until next month?
Josie:	That's all right. I understand. Next month will be fine.
Mr Miller:	OK. Is there anything else?
Josie:	No, that's all. Thanks, Mr Miller.
Mr Miller:	OK, Josie. I'll be in touch with you soon.

Comprehension Check!

❶ What are the problems with the apartment?
❷ What will Mr Miller do to help Josie?

Language Focus 2

Complaining and Responding to Complaints

(I'm) Sorry to disturb you.	Don't worry. That's all right. That's OK. How can I help you?
I'm calling about the apartment. I've come about my order.	What's the problem?
The boiler seems to be out of order. The shower isn't working (properly). The air conditioning won't turn on.	I'm (terribly/really/very) sorry about/for that. I do apologize. I'll look into the problem today. Shall I send a repair man today? Would you like me to call the maintenance man?

Talk 2

A Match the apartment problems with the consequences.

1. We're having problems with the oven.
2. The boiler isn't working.
3. There is no electricity.
4. We've lost the door key.
5. The washing machine is out of order.
6. The shower is leaking.
7. The air conditioning won't turn on.
8. The heating isn't working properly.

a. We are locked out.
b. There is water everywhere.
c. We can't switch on the lights.
d. We have no hot water.
e. The apartment is boiling hot.
f. We can't wash any clothes.
g. We can't cook any food.
h. The apartment is either too cold or too hot.

B Roleplay conversations with your partner between a tenant and a landlord. Use the information in **A**.

Example

A: I'm sorry to bother you. I'm calling about some problems with the apartment.
B: Really? What's the problem?
A: We're having problems with the oven. We can't cook any food. Could you possibly send someone to look at it?
B: Yes, of course.

Talk 3

Roleplay the situations with your partner.

❶

Student A: You applied to BAD Bank for a credit card. To check your salary, someone from the bank called your office and discussed your salary with one of your co-workers. Now, everyone in your department knows your salary. Call the bank to complain.

Student B: You work for BAD Bank. Respond to the customer's complaint and try to offer a solution.

❷

Student A: You work for Hopeless Air. Respond to the customer's complaint and try to offer a solution.

Student B: You took a flight with Hopeless Air last week. The outbound and return flights were both delayed, and you had to sleep overnight in the airport. Also, the airline lost your baggage. Call the airline to complain.

i Read

 Read the e-mail. What is the problem? What does the writer request?

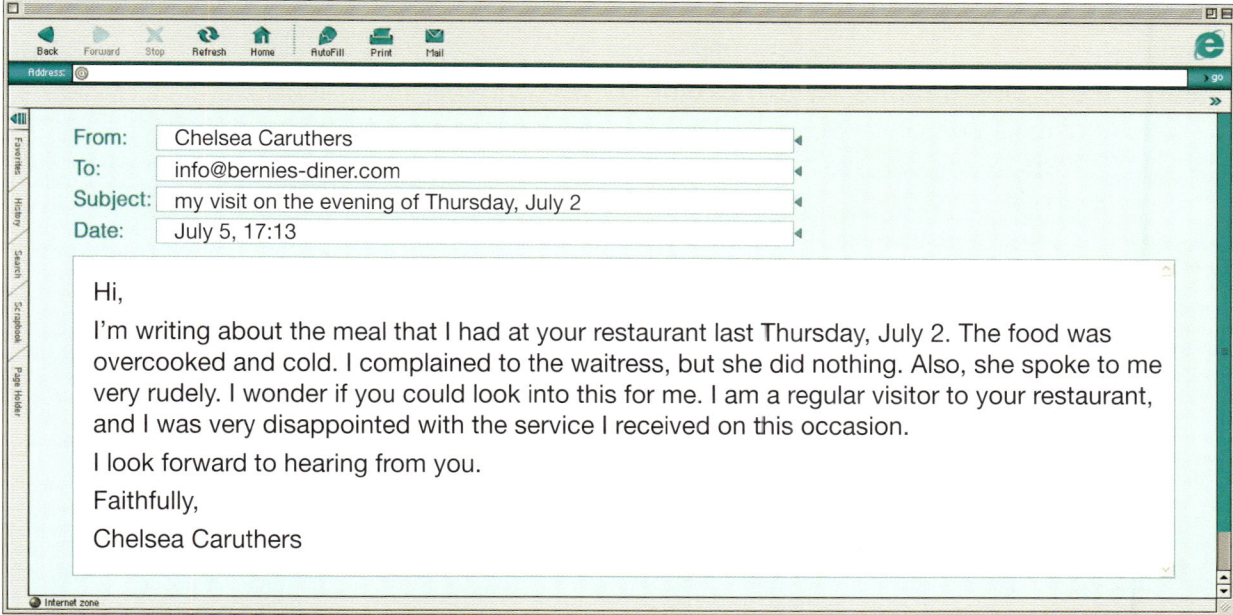

From: Chelsea Caruthers
To: info@bernies-diner.com
Subject: my visit on the evening of Thursday, July 2
Date: July 5, 17:13

Hi,

I'm writing about the meal that I had at your restaurant last Thursday, July 2. The food was overcooked and cold. I complained to the waitress, but she did nothing. Also, she spoke to me very rudely. I wonder if you could look into this for me. I am a regular visitor to your restaurant, and I was very disappointed with the service I received on this occasion.

I look forward to hearing from you.

Faithfully,

Chelsea Caruthers

 Discuss the questions with your partner.

1. How would you respond to the e-mail in **A**?
2. Have you ever been in a similar situation? What did you do?

i Write

 Talk with your partner about something that happened to you recently that you'd like to complain about.

 Write an e-mail to complain about the experience you talked about in **A**.

Lesson 15

How old were you?

Warm-Up

A Read the short biographies. Which person do you find the most interesting? Why?

My name is Laura. I was born in New York but grew up in Virginia. I graduated from college with a degree in health education and dance. I began working as an aerobics instructor six years ago. I have made many fitness DVDs, and now I teach other instructors and give lectures on fitness.

I'm Maria. I was born in Colombia but moved to the US when I was a kid. I wanted to be a movie director, so I began working for Universal Studios as an intern after college. I majored in cinematography. I have directed a few box office hits and won some awards. Now I am a world famous director.

Hi, I'm David. I am an English teacher in Korea. I was born in the UK and studied English literature at college. I moved to Korea three years ago to teach English and learn Korean culture. I enjoy teaching, and I am planning to open my own language school someday.

B Discuss the questions with your partner.

1. What do you think Laura liked to do when she was at college?
2. When did Maria move to the US? Where was she originally from?
3. What did David study at college? Why did he move to Korea?

C Complete the table, using information from the biographies in **A**.

	Laura	Maria	David
born in			
grew up in			
college major			
career			

Dialogue 1 *Listen to the dialogue and practice.*

Nathan: Wow, these are great pictures! They show your whole life history.
Melanie: I love them, too, especially the baby pictures. My mom says I smiled all the time when I was a baby. I didn't cry much. I was a happy baby.
Nathan: You look so cute! I guess you had many friends when you were a kid.
Melanie: Yes, I did. I liked to play hide-and-seek with my friends. And I played with dolls sometimes, especially when my friend Jenny came over to my house.
Nathan: You're on a family vacation in this picture. Where was this?
Melanie: I think it was Hawaii. I was nine. We had such a good time.
Nathan: Here you're singing. How old are you there?
Melanie: 15. I wanted to be a singer back then. But when I went to high school, I changed my mind. I decided to become a biologist thanks to my wonderful biology teacher.
Nathan: I see. Where did you go to high school?
Melanie: I went to Western High School in California. I loved that school.
Nathan: You are somewhere on campus in this picture. Where was this?
Melanie: It's near the residence hall. I lived in the dorm.

Comprehension Check!

1. What did Melanie like to do when she was a child?
2. What did she decide to do when she was in high school?
3. Where did she live?

Language Focus 1

Life History 1	
When were you born?	**I was born in** 1985.
Where were you born?	**I was born in** Anaheim, California.
What did you like to do when you were a kid?	**I liked to** play hide-and-seek.
Where did you go to high school?	**I went to high school in** San Diego.
Where did you live when you were at college?	**I lived** in the dorm.

Pronunciation

Linking Sounds Together

Discover Pronunciation!
Speakers often link sounds together.

Written	Spoken
turn off	tur_noff
wake up	way_cup
Can I have a bit of egg?	Ca-nI-ha-va-bi-to-fegg?

Practice Pronunciation!
Listen to the sentences and mark the linking. Then practice the sentences with your partner.

① Have a seat. ② I'll finish it in an hour. ③ That's enough.
④ Bring an apple and a book. ⑤ Come again anytime. ⑥ It's all over.

Talk 1

Ask your partner questions to complete the table.

What did you like to do ...	
When you were a kid?	
When you were in your teens?	
When you were a college student?	

Dialogue 2
Listen to the dialogue and practice.

Jenny: Hi, Roger. Have you done any research on Steven Spielberg?
Roger: Yes, I have. I have the information here. We can start working on our project now.
Jenny: Great. Let's start with his birth place. Where was he born?
Roger: He was born in Cincinnati, Ohio in 1946. He grew up in a few different states and graduated from high school in California.
Jenny: What did he like to do during his childhood and teenage years? Did he make movies?
Roger: He sure did. At the age of 13, he won a prize for a film he made. At 16, he wrote and directed his first independent film.
Jenny: Amazing! Where did he go to college?
Roger: He went to California State University in Long Beach, but he dropped out. However, he later finished a degree in 2002.
Jenny: It took so long for him to get his degree! What did he do after he dropped out of college?
Roger: He began his career as a professional director. He became famous when he made the movie *Jaws*. It was a huge box office hit.
Jenny: Right. And since then he has directed and produced so many great movies such as *Schindler's List*, *Jurassic Park*, and *Saving Private Ryan*.

Comprehension Check!
1. When did Steven Spielberg start making movies?
2. When did he begin his career as a professional director?

Talk 2

Read the short biographies to your partner. Can your partner guess who the people are?

1.
She studied chemistry at Oxford University and became a politician in 1959. She served as Prime Minister of the United Kingdom from 1979 to 1990.

2.
He was born in California and studied theater at college. He won consecutive Academy Awards for Best Actor for *Philadelphia* (1993) and *Forrest Gump* (1994).

3.
He was born in South Africa. As an anti-apartheid activist, he served 27 years in prison. He was elected President of South Africa in 1994, and served until 1999.

4.
She was born in Korea and began skating at the age of seven. She won a gold medal at the 2010 Winter Olympics, receiving the highest scores under the ISU Judging System.

5.
He grew up in Cupertino, California, and showed an interest in electronics from an early age. He eventually became co-founder, chairman, and chief executive officer of Apple Inc.

6.
She was a Roman Catholic nun who founded the Missionaries of Charity charitable organization in India. She devoted her life to looking after the sick, the dying, and the needy.

7.
He began his musical career at the age of five. He became a very successful singer-songwriter and record producer. He was called the King of Pop.

8.
She was born in Israel and moved to the US when she was three. She appeared in the film *Leon* in 1994. She won an Academy Award for her lead role as a ballerina in *Black Swan*.

Tom Hanks	Nelson Mandela	Yu-na Kim
Steve Jobs	Natalie Portman	Margaret Thatcher
Michael Jackson	Mother Teresa	

Language Focus 2

Life History 2	
Where did he grow up?	**He grew up in** Hawaii.
Where did he go to college?	**He went to** the University of Washington.
What did he do after he dropped out of college?	He began his career as an actor.

Talk 3
Track15-4

🎧 Listen to an interview with a chef and answer the questions.

① When did the chef first become interested in cooking?
② How old was he when he did his apprenticeship?
③ Where did he go to culinary school?
④ What did he do after he graduated from the school?

Lesson 15 • 127

i Read

A Read the resume. What kind of position do you think the person is applying for?

RESUME

Personal Details
First Name: Lisa   Surname: Chung
Date of Birth: 6/7/1980 (M/D/Y)   Place of Birth: New York, USA

Contact Details
E-Mail: lisac@umail.com   Phone: 201-555-5555 (Home) / 201-555-5567 (Mobile)

Academic Background

Institute	Major	Degree	Year
New York Culinary Institute	Culinary Arts Management	Bachelor's Degree	2005
The International Culinary School	Pastry and Baking Arts	Diploma	1999
Summit High School		Diploma	1998

Work Experience

Organization	Position	Location	Duration
Jay's Kitchen	Executive Cook	Edgewater, NJ	August 2005 – Present
Café Street	Pastry Chef	Brooklyn, NY	May 2000 – July 2005

B Discuss the questions with your partner.

1. How old was Lisa when she received her diploma from culinary school?
2. What was she doing at the same time as working as a pastry chef?
3. When do you think Lisa started studying at the New York Culinary Institute?

i Write

A Complete the resume, using your own personal information.

RESUME

Personal Details
First Name: _____ Surname: _____
Date of Birth: ___ / ___ / ___ (M/D/Y) Place of Birth: _____

Contact Details
E-Mail: _____ Phone: _____ (Home) / _____ (Mobile)

Academic Background

Institute	Major	Degree	Year

Work Experience

Organization	Position	Location	Duration

B Interview your partner to answer the questions.

1. What is your partner's full name?
2. Where was he/she born?
3. What did he/she do after graduating from high school?
4. Did he/she go to college? If he/she did, what was his/her major?
5. Does he/she work? If so, why did he/she choose their job?

Lesson 16: Are you going to change your career?

Warm-Up

A Complete the sentences to make them true for you. Use the ideas below, or your own ideas.

Future Plans

1. In the next ten years, I will _____.
2. In the next five years, I will _____.
3. This year, I will _____.
4. This month, I will _____.
5. This week, I will _____.
6. Tomorrow, I will _____.
7. Today, I will _____.

get a degree	go on vacation	go to the movies	have plastic surgery
study English	have children	meet my friends	live in a foreign country
travel abroad	win the lottery	get a job	open my own business
get married	eat out	move out	buy a house

B Discuss the questions with your classmates.

1. Does anyone have the same plans as you?
2. Is there a plan that everyone shares?

Dialogue 1 — Listen to the dialogue and practice.

Betty: Hello, John! How are you doing? I haven't seen you around lately.
John: Hi, Betty! Good to see you. I've been busy preparing my graduate school application.
Betty: Graduate school? That's awesome! Are you planning to do a master's degree?
John: Yes, I am. I've applied for several MBA programs. I want to develop my skills and abilities to be better at my job.
Betty: How awesome! So, what are you going to do when you graduate? Are you going to change your career?
John: I don't know yet. With the degree, I hope I'll have a better position with more pay. I'll see what's available.
Betty: I thought you wanted to set up your own business someday. Isn't that right?
John: I'd love to. I'm thinking of starting one in the next five years. But, before I do that, I want to get more experience in management.
Betty: Sounds like a plan. Good luck for your studies.
John: Thanks. I'll let you know if and when I get accepted.

Comprehension Check!

1. Why is John applying to graduate schools?
2. What is John planning to do after he gets an MBA degree?

Language Focus

Future Plans

Are you going to change your career?
Are you planning to go abroad?
I want to develop my skills and abilities.
I hope I'll have a better position with more pay.
I'm thinking of open**ing** my own business.
I'd love to have lunch with you.

Pronunciation

Consonant Replacements (Flap)

Discover Pronunciation!
When the letters *t* and *d* occur between vowels, they are often 'flapped'. The tip of the tongue touches the top of the mouth very quickly. The sound produced is similar to a very fast /d/.

letter	adding
bottle	middle
butter	medical
water	rider
What are you going to do? [**Whaddaya** going to do?]	**What do you** say? [**Whaddaya** say?]

Practice Pronunciation!

A Listen and practice.

❶ pu**tt**ing, pu**dd**ing ❷ la**tt**er, la**dd**er ❸ What's the ma**tt**er with the la**dd**er?
❹ **What are you** doing? ❺ **What do you** think? ❻ **What do you** eat?

B Practice the tongue twister with your partner.

Betty Botter bought a bit of butter.
The butter Betty Botter bought was a bit bitter
And made her batter bitter.
But a bit of better butter
Makes better batter.
So Betty Botter bought a bit of better butter,
Making Betty Botter's bitter batter better.

Talk 1

A Complete the sentences to make them true for you. Use the ideas below, or your own ideas.

1. After class, I will _____.
2. If I have a day off, I will _____.
3. Before I go to bed, I will _____.
4. When I'm on vacation, I will _____.
5. When the weather is sunny, I will _____.

go to the gym	take a trip to / travel to	spend time with family
watch movies	read books	meet my friends
surf the Internet	take a shower	go swimming/hiking
get some rest	have a party	go shopping

B Complete the sentences for your partner by asking him/her questions.

1. After class, my partner will _____.
2. If my partner has a day off, he/she will _____.
3. Before my partner goes to bed, he/she will _____.
4. When my partner's on vacation, he/she will _____.
5. When the weather is sunny, my partner will _____.

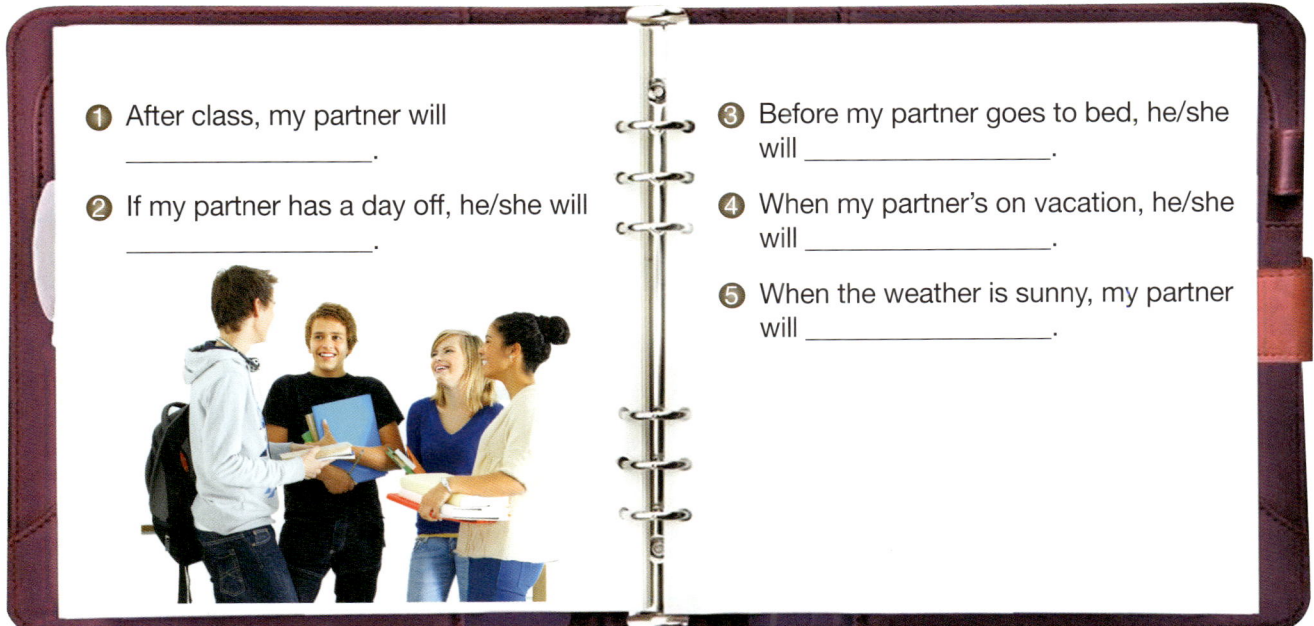

Dialogue 2   Listen to the dialogue and practice.

Scott: I heard you finally found a new apartment. When are you moving out?
Carol: I'm moving out this Saturday morning. Someone is moving in Saturday afternoon. I think I'll be packing until the last minute.
Scott: Wow, it sounds like a lot of work. Are you doing it all yourself?
Carol: Yes. But I'm moving into a furnished apartment, so I'm not taking any furniture with me. I think I can handle the rest.
Scott: What will you do with your furniture? Are you going to sell it?
Carol: I hope so. I posted an ad on the campus bulletin board.
Scott: Well I'll buy your sofa and kitchen table, including the chairs. How much do you want for those?
Carol: Let me see. [pause] How about 150 dollars? I'll also give you the bookshelf for free.
Scott: Great. It's a deal! Let me run to the bank and get some cash. When I come back, I'll pay for the furniture and help you with your packing.
Carol: Would you? That'd be nice. I appreciate it.

Comprehension Check!

❶ Where are Scott and Carol?
❷ What is Carol doing on Saturday morning?
❸ What is Scott going to do next?

Talk 2

A Make and respond to suggestions with your partner.

Making Suggestions	Accepting
• Would you like to go to the museum this Saturday? • How/What about going to the museum this Saturday? • Why don't we go to the museum this Saturday? • Let's go to the museum this Saturday.	• Yes, I'd like to / I'd love to. • Sure, that's a good idea. • That sounds great.

Refusing
• Oh, I'm sorry but I can't. I'm busy that day. • I'd love to, but I can't. I'm meeting my friends. • I'd like to, but I'm doing something else.

B Make and respond to more suggestions with your partner. Give reasons for refusing suggestions.

Accepting
A: Would you like to _____?
B: _____.
A: Great! Then I'll see you _____.

Refusing
A: How about _____?
B: _____.
A: Oh, that's too bad. _____.

Talk 3

🎧 Listen to the dialogues. Check (✓) whether the speakers accept or refuse the suggestions. Where suggestions are refused, write the reasons.

Dialogue	Accept	Refuse	Reasons
1			
2			
3			
4			

i Read

A Read someone's plans for the next ten years.

My Plans for the Next Ten Years

1 Celebrate tenth wedding anniversary
I got married just a month ago. Ten years from now, my husband and I will celebrate our tenth wedding anniversary. We will have a pretty box ready with a photo album of our memories and a love note. My husband and I will be very happy that we stood by each other.

2 Bring children up in loving environment
I will have two children: a boy and a girl. They will be eight and six in ten years since I am planning to have my first child in two years. They will enjoy their time at school, and have fun with their friends. They will be loved and well taken care of by their parents.

3 Move to a suburban area
As we love hiking and cycling, we will move to a suburban area with lots of open space. Our family will live in a safe and quiet neighborhood with great schools. I expect to meet wonderful people there, as I always have done in my life.

4 Travel
I will visit many countries around the world, both with my family and by myself in my job.

5 Helping others
My family will join an organization that helps the poor and needy. As volunteers, we will serve those who need our help.

6 Career
I will continue to pursue my career as an English teacher. In the next ten years, I will get a PhD in curriculum and instruction. I will train future English teachers and write books to help both students and educators.

B Discuss the questions with your partner.

1. What do you think of the plans in **A**? Are they similar to your plans?
2. If the person were living in your country, where would you recommend that he/she move to?
3. What organization in your country could the person join to help others?

i Write

Write your own plans for the next ten years. Then tell the class about your plans.

My Plans for the Next Ten Years

1. Marriage

2. Children

3. Move to

4. Travel

5. Career

6. Other

Listening Scripts

Lesson 5

[Talk 2]

Ⓐ Listen to the dialogue. What does the first speaker want to know? What advice does the second speaker give?

M: I want to go to college in the US. What does it take to get accepted to good colleges there?
W: Good colleges look for strong academic records, extracurricular activities, and good letters of recommendation.
M: Do I need to take a test?
W: Colleges have different test requirements. You may or may not have to take the SAT. Most colleges require international students to submit a score from an English language test.
M: When should I start planning for applying to college?
W: I advise you to start planning about two years in advance. Apply to colleges about a year before the course starts.

Lesson 13

[Talk 3]

Ⓐ Listen to the dialogue and check the correct options. Then add the appointment to the schedule.

Receptionist: Good morning. Dr Simpson's office. How may I help you?
William: Hello. I'd like to make an appointment to see the doctor. Can he see me next Tuesday?
Receptionist: I'm afraid not. He'll be out of the clinic all day. Can you come in on Monday afternoon?
William: No, I can't. Monday is a busy day for me. Is he free on Wednesday afternoon?
Receptionist: Let's see. [pause] How about 3 pm? Will that be OK with you?
William: Yes. Wednesday at 3 pm is good for me.
Receptionist: Sounds good. Your full name and phone number, please.
William: My first name is William, and my surname is Carter: C-A-R-T-E-R. My phone number is 332-7086.

Ⓑ Listen again and complete the dialogue. Then practice the dialogue with your partner.

Lesson 15

[Talk 3]

Ⓐ Listen to an interview with a chef and answer the questions.

Interviewer: When did you first realize that you wanted to become a chef?
Chef: My family has a long history in the business. Growing up in a family like mine, cooking came naturally to me.
Interviewer: Who influenced you the most to become a chef?
Chef: My uncle and my mother. They ran a restaurant together, so by the time I was five, I was spending most of my free time in the kitchen.
Interviewer: Where did you go to culinary school?
Chef: I went to Cordon Bleu in France. Before that, I did a two-year apprenticeship at the age of 15 at a four-star hotel. I also learned a great deal from my experience at my family's restaurant.
Interviewer: After you graduated from the school, what did you do?
Chef: I did an internship for six months at a restaurant in Paris. Then I got a job at a hotel.

Lesson 16

[Talk 3]

Listen to the dialogues. Check whether the speakers accept or refuse the suggestions. Where suggestions are refused, write the reasons.

Dialogue 1
W: Would you like to go out for some ice cream after school? Today's 20% off day!
M: Really? OK, I'd be happy to go with you.
W: All right. See you later.

Dialogue 2
M: I'm going to have a party tomorrow. Will you come?
W: I'd like to, but I can't. I have a family gathering to go to.
M: I see. Well, maybe next time, then.

Dialogue 3
M: I'm going to sign up for skydiving class. Why don't you join me?
W: I'm sorry, but I can't. I'm afraid of heights.
M: Oh, I didn't know that. Then let me find a different class for you.

Dialogue 4
W: If you're free tomorrow night, would you like to go to a ballet performance with me?
M: Yes, I'd love to. What time shall we meet?
W: Let's meet at 6:00 pm and have dinner first. The ballet starts at 7:30.

Notes